NOTHING EXISTS THAT IS NOT ŚIVA

NOTHING EXISTS THAT IS NOT ŚIVA

Commentaries on the

Śiva Sūtra, Vijñānabhairava, Gurugītā,

and Other Sacred Texts

by

SWAMI MUKTANANDA

A SIDDHA YOGA PUBLICATION
PUBLISHED BY SYDA FOUNDATION

Published by SYDA Foundation
371 Brickman Rd., P.O. Box 600, South Fallsburg, New York 12779, USA

On the front cover: The photograph depicts the Himalayas of Kashmir, the region in North India where a great many of the scriptures quoted here were written.

Acknowledgments

This revised and expanded edition is a result of the concerted efforts of a great many dedicated and talented people, most especially the editors and translators of *Siddha Meditation*, on which this book is based. A retranslation of Swami Muktananda's manuscript from the original Hindi was done by Śrī Pratap Yande, with assistance from Anand Mundra, who translated and rendered the poetry, and Dayavrat Sharma, who checked the manuscript against the earlier English editions. Prof. Paul Muller-Ortega and Dr. Hans Turstig were Sanskrit advisors, and Patrick Tierney translated Swami Shantananda's introduction from Spanish. Valerie Sensabaugh was text coordinator; Cheryl Crawford was designer; Stéphane Dehais and Shambhavi Sachs were typesetters; Martin Epstein was Devanagari typesetter; and Osnat Shurer and Sushila Traverse oversaw production. The cover photograph was taken by Arthur Nichols. To these and the many others who generously offered their assistance, we extend grateful appreciation.

Peggy Bendet, Editor

Printed in the United States of America

97 98 99 00 01 02 03 5 4 3 2 1

Parts 1 and 3 are new translations from the original Hindi manuscript, which was published in English as *Siddha Meditation: Commentaries on the Shiva Sutras and Other Sacred Texts* in 1975 in Oakland, California; in 1977 in Ganeshpuri, India; and in 1979 in South Fallsburg, New York.

Library of Congress Cataloging-in-Publication Data
Muktananda, Swami, 1908-
Nothing exists that is not Śiva : commentaries on the Śiva Sūtra, Vijñānabhairava, Gurugītā, and other sacred texts / by Swami Muktananda.
p. cm.
"A Siddha Yoga publication."
Rev. and expanded ed. of: Siddha meditation. 1979.
ISBN 0-911307-56-7 (pbk. : alk. paper)
1. Vasugupta. Śivasūtra. 2. Kashmir Śaivism — Sacred books. 3. Kashmir Śaivism — Doctrines. I. Muktananda, Swami, 1908- Siddha meditation. II. Title.
BL1281.1592.V38M85 1997
294.5'95—dc21 97-22811

TABLE OF CONTENTS

PART ONE

Śiva Sūtra

Pratyabhijñāhṛdayam

Spanda Kārikā

Svacchanda Tantra

PART TWO

Vijñānabhairava

PART THREE

Gurugītā

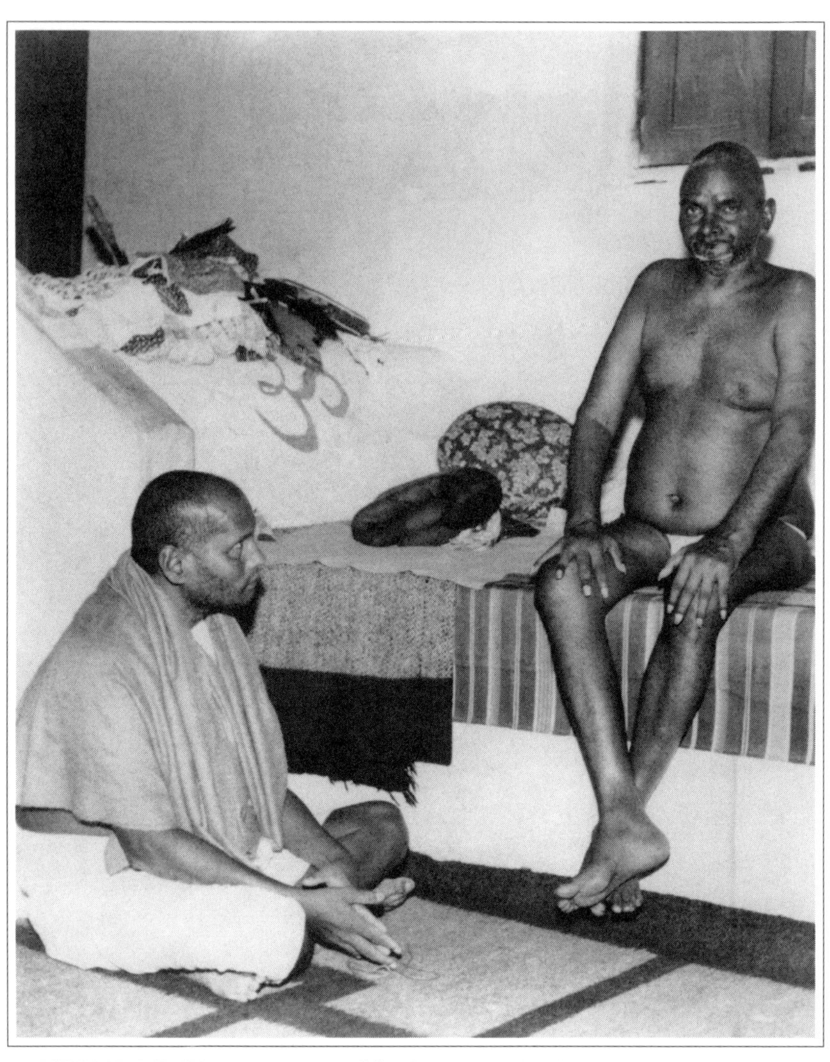

SWAMI MUKTANANDA *with his Guru* BHAGAWAN NITYANANDA

INVOCATION

I bow to Nityananda, whose essential form exists at all times, who dwells in all things, who illumines all things, and who has become absolute Consciousness. He is himself light and has expanded outward in play; he is full of bliss.

Being the grace-bestowing power of the supreme Lord, he is the Guru to the disciple. As sunlight conquers darkness, his spontaneous nature overcomes for his disciples the impurity-covered world of change. To fulfill the four basic goals of his devotees[1] and to foster the inner and outer play of Consciousness, he has assumed a body that houses the mystery of shaktipat. He is without decay or destruction. He is the inner light and the goal of mantra. He is supreme Consciousness itself. He is Gurudev Nityananda. I bow to him with the infinite feeling of surrender and in perfect I-consciousness.

Having merged his individual existence in the Self before the beginning of time, he effortlessly liberates by his grace. Since the sunrise of liberation brings the aim of outer joy and the peaceful bliss of the Self, he has spontaneously become Muktananda, the bliss of freedom. He is Nityananda, the joyful exuberance of Consciousness.

> He who is eternal Bliss, full of Truth and Consciousness;
> he whose work it is to end the disciple's world of change;
> he who is the body of Consciousness,
> a body sporting for the sake of devotees;
> such a one is your Nityananda, O Muktananda.

SWAMI MUKTANANDA

The universe is made up of the seer and the seen, the perceiver and the perceived. Its processes—creation, sustenance, and dissolution—are presided over by Rudra and other deities. All creatures are subject to these same processes. Supreme Śiva, the *tattva* (principle), is everlasting. All gods and all creatures originate in it and merge into it when they dissolve. The universe arises as a throb of that reality and abides in it. It emanates its rays of *śakti* in total freedom. These rays are the alphabet from *a* to *kṣa.*

The Śiva *tattva* is immortal, the transcendent vibratory principle. The universe, in undifferentiated unity, lives in its very being, though appearing to be different from it. It is conscious and nondual, the source of infinite bliss. It is the highest luminous truth, Śaṅkara, the all-pervasive Self of all.

The first aphorism of the *Śiva Sūtra* is *caitanyam ātmā,* "The *ātman,* or Self, is Consciousness." The Self unfolds its countless powers when it sets out to create a universe and manifests as the subject (perceiver) and the object (perceived). Though the cosmos contains the twofold division of seer and seen, still it is a unity since there is not a single object in it that cannot be apprehended by Consciousness or illumined by it. An object that is not amenable to knowledge (perception) cannot exist.

The functional aspects of Citi, the rays of the light of Consciousness, are present in all directions, everywhere. The nature of Consciousness is to be ready to know, to know, and to make known. The mode of Consciousness is to fill all objects, perceptions, and activities while remaining free. Only Paraśiva, supreme truth, is thus free. It governs all the *tattvas* from earth up to Śiva.

Paraśiva is eternal, pervasive, formless. It activates everything. It is the soul of the universe—supremely pure, completely full, the conscious Self. It does not change, though it manifests as space, time, and form. It is the Consciousness within the spirit within the heart, and it is the same as the Consciousness without. Right knowledge is the direct awareness of the pervasiveness of Consciousness within and without. Such an undifferentiated understanding brings worldly fulfillment and spiritual liberation, perfection, realization, and peace. It lacks only bondage and suffering.

The truth is that to realize the Self is to get what we already have. There is nothing apart from Śiva. There is nothing other than Śiva. Whatever there is, is Śiva. To be aware of Paraśiva is to be fearless and free in the Self. There is nothing that is not Śiva; there is no place that is not Śiva; there is no time that is not Śiva; there is no state that is not Śiva. Not a single thought-wave can arise separate from Śiva. To be aware of this is to be aware of Śiva. Here, there, wherever you look, whatever you think—it is all Śiva. The *Śiva Sūtra* is alive with this divine awareness.

The perfectly nondual awareness of Śiva is available by Guru's grace, by the favor of Nityananda, by the love of Śiva. We must worship, remember, and understand Śiva by becoming Śiva. This is the path of Nityananda, the path given by the Guru. It is nothing new; it is not a sect or a cult, not the monopoly of a single people or a single land. It is the religion of all countries, all religions, all societies, all people.

Śiva teaches that the Self is supreme bliss. The path to Śiva culminates not in the void but in the bliss that transcends the void. Meditation on the Self is the means to this consummation, and shaktipat makes it possible. The Being that is immanent and transcendent and yet undifferentiated is the highest realization. Remembering the all-pervasive Consciousness seated in the heart, we bow to Śiva—*Oṃ Namaḥ Śivāya.*

When you yourself are true, then the Guru, the mantra, and Śiva are also true. To be true is to be good; to be true is to be beautiful.

Your own,

स्वामी मुक्तानंद

Swami Muktananda

INTRODUCTION

In *Nothing Exists That Is Not Śiva,* Swami Muktananda presents commentaries on aphorisms and stanzas of the scriptures he read and quoted most frequently. Seeing the harmony between Baba Muktananda's understanding of these scriptures and his direct knowledge of spiritual life, we can know that he has fulfilled one of the scriptural requirements of a true Guru as stated in the *Muṇḍaka Upaniṣad*: he is a *śrotriyaṃ brahmaniṣṭham*; he is a knower of the scriptures and is established in the realization of God.

The majority of the commentaries included here were written in early 1973 at Gurudev Siddha Peeth, the mother ashram of Siddha Yoga, in Ganeshpuri, India. In the mornings, from 5:30 to 7:00, while the ashram students were chanting the *Gurugītā* in the Temple, Baba would sit alone or with his dogs on the ledge just outside his house, his favorite place in the ashram courtyard. There he peacefully wrote his commentaries on the scriptures of Śaivism, both the esoteric texts of Kashmir—*Śiva Sūtra, Pratyabhijñāhṛdayam,* and others—and the *Gurugītā,* the devotional hymn that the ashram residents were at that moment singing. By the time the devotees had finished the morning recitation and were leaving the Temple, Baba had already completed that day's commentaries. Later the commentaries were translated from Hindi to English, and sometimes they were read aloud in the courtyard before lunch, while Baba gave darshan. Many of these writings appeared in the Gurudev Siddha Peeth *Newsletter* before they were compiled and published, in the summer of 1975, under the title *Siddha Meditation.*

In preparing this current volume for publication, one of Baba's longtime disciples Śrī Pratap Yande and others studied Baba's original manuscript along with the English text. As a result, this edition includes an invocation by Baba and several additional commentaries, all of which appear here for the first time. Also in many places the language has been amended to reflect more closely Baba's original words.

This volume also marks the first publication of Baba Muktananda's expansive rendering of eighteen verses of the *Vijñāna-bhairava,* a Śaiva text he was reading daily in the last few months of his life. These verses comprise part 2. In his very clear expositions, which he wrote in 1979, Baba focuses on the first of the *dhāraṇās,* the concentration exercises, that describe meditation on the mantra *Haṃsa,* "I am That." By understanding the first *dhāraṇā* on *Haṃsa,* Baba used to explain, one can understand and master all of the 112 *dhāraṇās* in the *Vijñānabhairava.* Baba had such respect for this *dhāraṇā* in particular that on many occasions he initiated students in this practice, and in 1978 he wrote a small book, *I Am That,* in which he explained how to meditate with the awareness of *Haṃsa.*

The Vision of a Siddha

When *Siddha Meditation* was first published, it was a milestone for the Siddha Yoga students. For the first time, Baba Muktananda had put down on paper the remarkable teachings of Kashmir Śaivism, which his students had glimpsed in his talks and books, particularly his spiritual autobiography *Play of Consciousness.* In those days only a handful of scholars knew of Kashmir Śaivism, and translations of Śaivite scriptures were rare and not readily available.

In my first reading of this book, I was stunned by its magnificent view of the world, of life, of a human being's place in the order of creation. The vision Baba Muktananda is offering us in these pages is the vision of a Siddha. A Siddha, a "fulfilled" being—which is what this Sanskrit term means—is someone who has merged his sense of individuality with the supreme Consciousness of God. A Siddha's experience is that God, his own inner Self, and the world constitute an indivisible unity, full of joy. The perception of a Siddha is completely bathed in divine radiance.

One of the renowned masters of Kashmir, Maheśvarānanda, who probably lived at the end of the twelfth century, describes how the light of divine Consciousness emanates from the center of our being, like a wave in the ocean, and flows in surges of delight through all our senses to capture the impressions of the world. That same light then brings those impressions inward and, through the agency of the mind, leaves them as offerings for the enjoyment of the luminous Self.

A Siddha is fully conscious of this light of divinity; he perceives the world as being permeated by the splendor of God. His state, even in the daily experience of mundane activities, is the most elevated state a human being can attain. The fulfillment of a Siddha lies in the constant experience that nothing exists anywhere that does not reveal the divine luminosity, an observation from the *Svacchanda Tantra* that Baba notes in these pages and from which this volume takes its new name. This vision might seem unattainable. Far from it: the purpose of *Nothing Exists That Is Not Śiva* is to illumine the path by which we can attain the state of a Siddha and, above all, to remind us that this state exists in its potential within each one of us.

Baba Muktananda was not only a fulfilled being; he was a Guru as well, a spiritual Master of the highest order. In this book we see how Baba exhorts, explains, and guides, how he teaches us the ways in which we can reach what he himself reached.

The Key to Meditation

There is in India an old story that tells how God hid the key to heaven in a place where people couldn't find it: in the human heart. Baba had entered that inner kingdom and obtained the key to open the door for others. Baba called this key shaktipat—in Sanskrit, it's *śaktipāta*—which literally means "descent of energy," referring to the divine energy that a Siddha Guru can transmit at will into a seeker, thereby awakening the seeker's own inner power. Baba used to say that the true secret of meditation is this inner awakening that takes place through contact with a Siddha Guru. In this book, we see frequent references to shaktipat as the most efficacious means to meditate, to unfold our latent virtues, to obtain lasting happiness, and to realize God within ourselves. This initiation, received from a Siddha Guru—like Baba Muktananda or his spiritual heir, Swami Chidvilasananda, the present head of the Siddha Yoga lineage—is the distinctive characteristic of Siddha Yoga as a spiritual path.

The subtle energy that is unlocked when a person receives

shaktipat is known as Kuṇḍalinī Śakti. In the scriptures of India, this tremendous force, which resides in all human beings in a potential form, is spoken of as the beneficent Goddess, the supreme power of God, who is lying asleep within us. Once Kuṇḍalinī is awakened, She begins to move through the seeker, purifying one on all levels, physical and subtle, and in the course of time, leading one to the experience of the immense sweetness that lies hidden within one's own being.

I used to be fascinated by the descriptions of ecstatic love in the biographies of Śrī Ramakrishna, Anandamayi Ma, and many other great mystics. I would wonder, "What happens to someone who has entered into an intimate relationship with God? What does it feel like to be in that state?" Soon after receiving shaktipat from Baba, I began to feel euphoria in meditation. It welled up from deep within me and flowed throughout my body. "This is the love of the mystics!" I said to myself, surprised it was happening to *me*. My mind, drawn to this tenderness, forgot its concerns and fantasies. As I continued to meditate, the waves of love became stronger. My body became engulfed by ecstasy, tears of joy fell, and I found myself wanting nothing other than this pure love.

In time, the intensity of this love took the form of a serene equanimity, allowing me to see the inner light of the conscious Self, pure and without attachment, as the origin and support of everything that exists. It was this experience, initiated by the Guru, that gave me the certainty that the sweetness of the Self is the very presence of God.

God as the Self Within

My own experience of inner divinity, which is shared by countless people who have received shaktipat from Baba and from Gurumayi Chidvilasananda, reflects the fundamental message of Siddha Yoga. This is contained in a statement Baba Muktananda made again and again during his life:

> Meditate on your Self.
> Worship your Self.
> Love your Self.
> God dwells within you as you.

SWAMI CHIDVILASANANDA

The Indian scriptures, which Baba Muktananda knew well, affirm that the highest goal of each human being is to have an experience of God as the Self within. Yet this most subtle experience, which is clearly the purpose of meditation and, indeed, of all spiritual practice, is possibly the most difficult to describe. What vocabulary can we use? The experience is not something we *achieve* or *reach* or *attain*; all of these terms, although they're widely used in mystical literature, show a partial understanding. The Self is not something we *have* (or *lack*); we *are* the Self. The most accurate perspective would be that the Self wears a physical body, the way someone might wear a suit of clothing. But, then, what is it that happens that allows us to have this experience? And to whom does it happen?

In describing this most exalted experience, Baba employs a precise Sanskrit term from Kashmir Śaivism: *pratyabhijñā*, recognition. We recognize, that is, we return to the cognition of that which we truly are. In forgetting our identity, we have identified with the suit of clothing, with the superficial and relative appearance of our existence: our body, gender, and name; our skills and idiosyncrasies. When we come to the state of recognition, we remember our most profound identity, our identity with the supreme Self. In this sense, recognition is the highest knowledge—not information, not logical or even philosophical knowledge, but the direct experience of the Self.

Recognition of the Self inevitably transforms the ways in which we view ourselves and the world. It changes the habit of judging ourselves and others based on appearances. It can remove the doubts and patterns of behavior that keep us running in the same circles again and again. It can halt the endless cycle of ups and downs we experience as a part of existence. Once we have this vision, we can embrace the deepest truth of our life. *Nothing Exists That Is Not Śiva* has the power to stir this spiritual awakening in us. On each page, we can almost hear Baba urging us, "Wake up! Look at the marvelous world we live in. Recognize the divine power that resides within you!"

The Auspicious One

In speaking of Śaivism, the question arises, who is Śiva? In India, there are many answers: "the god of destruction," "the compassionate lord of yoga," or even "the deity who meditates on Mount Kailasa, seated on a tiger skin with serpents around his neck and the river Gaṅgā emerging from the locks of his tangled hair." The Purāṇas narrate the difficulties and austerities Pārvatī undertook in order to marry this detached ascetic, the unusual birth of his two sons Kārttikeya and Gaṇeśa, and other exploits that demonstrate a deity who is in complete control of his senses, a destroyer of negative forces, the ideal practitioner of yoga and meditation, and at the same time, a being capable of enjoying mundane pleasures without identifying with them. This is the Śiva of popular devotion, whose images are seen in innumerable temples throughout India.

The Śiva of the Āgamas, the revealed scriptures that describe the Śaiva tradition, finds His origin in the aspects described above, but our view of Him has been expanded to the ultimate degree of depth and breadth. His name means "the auspicious one." This Śiva is the ultimate reality, the light of Consciousness, who manifests as the cosmos, penetrates it as the being of all things, and dissolves it again within Himself. Given this, what could be more auspicious than to attain the supreme bliss of Śiva?

In Śaivism, Śiva and Pārvatī are seen as personifications of the two fundamental aspects of the supreme Being. Śiva represents light, the principle of existence and being, and Pārvatī (or Śakti) represents the primordial energy, supreme will, and absolute ecstasy. As Śiva's power, Śakti plays a principal role in Śaivism—the attainments of yoga and meditation are identified with Śakti.

Śakti, for instance, is the power of Consciousness—that is to say, She is that which knows itself. Metaphorically, one could say that Śakti is the mirror in which Śiva sees Himself and exclaims with delight, "I am!" In addition to being Self-consciousness, Śakti is the creative energy, conscious of everything She has created. Through Her expression as Kuṇḍalinī, it is Śakti that brings about one's full recognition of the Self.

It must be noted, however, that this Kashmiri branch of Śaivism is utterly monistic; Śiva and Śakti are distinguished as separate principles only for the sake of explication. In reality, the sages of Śaivism say, there is only one principle.

What is the importance of knowing all this? The attributes of the supreme Self are also a description of each and every one of us. Thus, Śiva and Śakti are the fundamental aspects of our own Self. One could say, "I exist because I am Śiva; I am aware of myself and my world because I am Śakti." The Self establishes its presence without the support of thought or speech, with the knowledge of the subtle vibration that is experienced as *ahaṃ,* "I am."

In the ancient writings of India, it is customary to begin a text with the principal theme of the work. In his first commentary here, Baba establishes the purpose of *Nothing Exists That Is Not Śiva* by explaining the first aphorism of the *Śiva Sūtra, caitanyam ātmā,* "The Self is Consciousness." The realization of the nature of the *ātman,* the Self, Baba tells us, is the beginning, middle, and end of the spiritual quest.

When we enter into deep meditation, the power of Śakti awakened in us by the Guru gently draws our attention inward, toward the Self. We leave behind our identification with the physical body, with the mind and the personality, and, ultimately, even with the void of deep sleep. We arrive, finally, at the luminous region within, where the light of supreme Consciousness radiates in all directions, reverberating with the knowledge of *aham,* "I am." When our awareness becomes established in this eternal *I am,* which is the innermost Self, we gain the sovereignty, the supreme independence of the Self. In this freedom, without attachments or expectations, exists pure bliss, pure love.

The Means and the Goal

To illustrate the dynamic of the spiritual process of Siddha Yoga, Baba uses a very simple image. The spiritual journey, he says, is like a bird that needs two wings to fly: one wing represents the power of grace, and the other wing, self-effort. Grace is activated in the seeker with the awakening of Kuṇḍalinī. Baba writes:

> As a result of the transmission of Śakti, the power of Consciousness, meditation comes spontaneously, and innumerable *kriyās,* including *āsanas, mudrās,* and different kinds of *prāṇāyāma,* take place. The seeker turns within. Awareness of the inner Self

> begins to throb all the time within him. To stay with this awareness is the right effort for the seeker.

In reality, grace is the source of all the experiences of meditation: spontaneous physical movements, inner visions, exquisite sounds, the delectable taste of subtle nectar, inspiration and revelation, visits to other worlds or from beings who come from those worlds, the ecstasy of pure love, the transformation of one's own character, and most important of all, the experience of the presence of the Self within. All of this is a gift of grace, a gift of the Guru.

With so much being given, one might wonder, "Where is the room for self-effort? Is there anything left for me to do?" Yet Siddha Yoga meditation requires more of us than our simply sitting down and waiting for blessings to rain upon us. According to Baba, right effort in spiritual practice is that which "involves the complete identification of the meditating seeker and the object of meditation." When we identify with the object of meditation—the Self—this *ātmabhāva,* or Self-awareness, then reveals the essential character of the practice, be it mantra repetition, selfless service, chanting sacred texts, contemplation of the words of great beings, acts of charity, and so on. In other words, right effort requires something more than just performing spiritual practices; it is an inner posture we adopt, a resolve to see the world from the point of view of Śiva. Baba comments on a stanza by the sage Somānanda, *śivena śivasādhanaḥ,* "Śiva is realized by means of Śiva," saying:

> You should discard concepts such as "world," "bound soul," and "evil thoughts," and practice identification with Śiva. Live in the awareness of your Śivahood, your divinity. You are Śiva's. Become Śiva and nothing but Śiva.

The leitmotif of *Nothing Exists That Is Not Śiva* is this apparent paradoxical polarity: You are Śiva; become Śiva. You are the Self; attain the Self. You are pure; purify your understanding. Meditation is the work of grace; practice meditation. Baba indicates again and again that the sadhana he shows us encompasses all polarities. We are searching for God, and yet at the same time we *are* God. We use techniques for spiritual practice, and yet no technique is going to give us what we already have.

In the experience of *pratyabhijñā,* recognition of one's Self, unfolds the awareness "I am the means, and I am the goal." For a seeker, right effort is to adopt this posture, radical though it may seem, contrary though it may be to the way we see ourselves. Just this shift in our awareness gives us the impetus to follow the magnificent perspective of sadhana that Baba offers us:

> God forgets His own true nature and looks for God. God worships God. God meditates on God, and God is trying to find God. It is God who questions and God who answers.

To think of ourselves as Śiva is not an impractical, utopian daydream, but the yogic practice of aligning ourselves with the same divine power that propels sadhana. The rewards of this subtle effort can be astonishing.

One of Baba's longtime devotees once related an experience of putting this philosophical stance into practice when she was working as a waitress. She detested this job, she told me, because she felt the atmosphere of the restaurant wasn't "yogic"—the people she served were often smoking, drinking, and just generally indulging in the pleasures and distractions of worldly life. Whenever she could, this young woman would escape to a quiet corner and pour over her copy of this book. Baba's message that everything in the world is a manifestation of divine Consciousness was like a balm for her depressed spirit.

She said that on one occasion she was particularly inspired by Baba's words. She picked up her tray with unaccustomed enthusiasm, walked into the restaurant's dining room—and found it had been transformed as if by an act of magic. The plate of oysters she retrieved from the kitchen shone with rays of pale blue light. That same shimmering light pervaded the shiny bottles of beer, the cigarettes with their undulating curls of smoke, the tables, the walls, the people—everything glowed with the light of supreme Consciousness! The young woman stood stock-still, her feet anchored to the floor with waves of bliss coursing through her body. The restaurant had become a fragment of heaven that had descended upon earth.

This young woman's experience is a perfect example of *pratyabhijñā,* the spontaneous recognition of the face of God in His varied creation. The teachings of Śaivism maintain that any perception, any experience can serve as a doorway to this recognition of divinity. And as this incident illustrates, the pages of this very book can open that door for us, even in the most unlikely circumstances. The Guru's words, like living mantras, are filled with the illuminative power of his own state.

The Guru

In the first two parts of *Nothing Exists That Is Not Śiva,* Baba speaks of the role of right effort, the path the disciple travels after initiation. In the third part, Baba describes the tremendous importance of grace in this journey to liberation.

Here Baba gives free expression to his favorite subject: the Guru. Baba dearly loved his Guru, Bhagawan Nityananda. As Baba said many times, the Guru was the source of everything he achieved in his spiritual life. For him there was nothing greater, nothing more sublime or exalted than the grace of his Guru. To hear Baba speak of his Bhagawan Nityananda was to glimpse the very presence of this great Siddha. Baba Muktananda had merged his identity with that of his Guru to such an extent that many of Baba's disciples were able to see the form of Bhagawan Nityananda within the physical form of Baba.

In the third part of *Nothing Exists That Is Not Śiva,* Baba takes us on an excursion through selected stanzas of the *Gurugītā,* "The Song of the Guru," a beautiful, praiseful text that describes the sublimity and glory of the spiritual Master. In describing the Guru, Baba becomes the perfect devotee, finding lyrical expression for his love of his Guru.

As a context for devotion to the Guru, one must understand that the Guru is not just a personality or a physical form. This is something Baba always vigorously emphasized. As Baba writes in his invocation to this book:

> Being the grace-bestowing power of the supreme Lord, he is the Guru to the disciple. As sunlight conquers darkness, his

> spontaneous nature overcomes for his disciples the impurity-covered world of change. To fulfill the four basic goals of his devotees and to foster the inner and outer play of Consciousness, he has assumed a body that houses the mystery of shaktipat. He is without decay or destruction. He is the inner light and the goal of mantra. He is supreme Consciousness itself.

The Guru is Śiva, manifest in a human form that has been purified in the fire of sadhana. Such a being exists for the sole purpose of serving as initiator and guide to those who are not yet established in *pratyabhijñā,* the recognition of their own inherent divinity.

The essence of the disciple's relationship to the spiritual Master is devotion. Baba says that the intensity of one's devotion for the Guru is itself the fire that consumes impurities, opens the hidden inner kingdom, and grants profound knowledge. And yet true devotion, Baba tells us, is saturated with the same sublime vision that distinguishes right effort in any spiritual endeavor: one recognizes—re-cognizes, or knows again—that God, Guru, and one's own inner Being are all aspects of the same divine Consciousness. Once again, we return; we close the circle. Then what is seen at the beginning of sadhana as duality, as an apparent separation between disciple and Guru, becomes a recognition that we are indivisibly one. In loving the Guru, the disciple is, in reality, loving his own true Self, and by his *gurubhakti,* his devotion for the spiritual Master, the disciple embraces God, all of humanity, and all of creation.

Swami Shantananda
Shree Muktananda Ashram
South Fallsburg, New York
April 1997

NOTHING EXISTS THAT IS NOT

ŚIVA

PART ONE

Śiva Sūtra, Pratyabhijñāhṛdayam, and Other Śaiva Texts

A NOTE ON THE TEXTS

The texts upon which Swami Muktananda comments in part 1 belong to the tradition of *advaita* or nondualistic Śaivism of Kashmir. This region of North India saw a remarkable unfoldment of philosophical activity between the eighth and thirteenth centuries of the common era, centered around Śiva as embodiment of the supreme reality. What we know as Kashmir Śaivism is the elaboration of a number of great sages on older revealed scriptures called Āgamas or Tantras. In selecting texts for commentary, a long-established practice among the spiritual teachers of India, Baba chose those passages that reflect his experience of the spiritual journey and the path that he set forward for his own disciples.

The *Śiva Sūtra* ("The Aphorisms of Śiva"), which forms by far the largest part of the commentary, lays the foundation of this tradition. It is recorded that one night the sage Vasugupta had a dream in which Lord Śiva revealed to him that certain teachings were inscribed on the bottom of a large boulder lying on the shore of a brook at the foot of Mahadev Mountain. The sage was told that if he touched the rock, it would turn over of its own accord and reveal the inscription. Accordingly, the next day he found what is now known as the *Śiva Sūtra,* revealed by the Lord out of compassion for a world in spiritual deprivation. This event took place before the end of the eighth century in the forests near the city of Shrinagar, in Kashmir.

Other works in this section include the *Spanda Kārikā* ("The Stanzas on Divine Vibration"), also written by Vasugupta or perhaps, as some erudites prefer to believe, by his disciple Kallaṭa. It dates from the end of the eighth or beginning of the ninth century and is meant to be an expansion of the teachings contained in the *Śiva Sūtra.* Baba also refers to the *Śivadṛṣṭi* ("The Vision of Śiva") by Somānanda, who lived at the end of the ninth century. We find as well quotes from the *Īśvarapratyabhijñā Kārikā* ("The Stanzas on the Recognition of the Lord"), written at the beginning of the tenth century by Somānanda's disciple, Utpaladeva, where *pratyabhijñā,* the spontaneous recognition of the Self, is the central axis of the practice of yoga. Swami Muktananda pays particular attention to the *Pratyabhijñāhṛdayam* ("The Heart of Recognition"), a small compendium containing the fundamental teachings of the tradition, written in the early eleventh century by Kṣemarāja, a disciple of Abhinavagupta, who was the foremost among all the Śaivite masters of Kashmir.

Most of the scriptural passages chosen for this book are in aphoristic forms that may sound cryptic to modern ears: "Yogic realizations are marvelous," "Knowledge is food," "The power of will is the maiden Umā." In India, the Guru might ask his students to contemplate these statements or he might lecture on them, expanding the students' understanding of their meaning. The commentarial approach taken here is, therefore, perfectly in keeping with tradition.

—*Swami Shantananda*

चैतन्यमात्मा

caitanyam ātmā

Consciousness is the Self.

Śiva Sūtra 1.1

He who dwells in all places, things, and times as one with all; who always consciously walks, consciously talks, consciously sees, hears, gives, and takes; He who is the Self of all and is capable of doing all without any instruments of doing; who dwells in all yet is separate from all; who is with all yet friend to none; that one, utterly free, illuminating everything, is called *caitanya,* Consciousness. He is the Self.

Though He is nothing, He becomes everything necessary at the proper time. He holds without hands, walks without feet, sees without eyes, talks without tongue, and hears without ears. He is neither man nor woman, yet conducts the workings of the world taking the form of man and woman.

Such a one, filled with Consciousness, is *caitanya ātman,* the Self. Though the very essence of formlessness, He lives on the far shore of formlessness.

Like sparks arising spontaneously and infinitely from a blazing fire, infinite universes rise and set of their own accord out of Him, yet remain one with Him. Even as these infinite universes rise and set from Him and in Him, He remains supremely peaceful, supremely free from agitation.

That inner Consciousness is the Self.

To create forms or to have created forms, to be created or to continue to be created—for Him these are all natural and spontaneous activities, not artificial. He becomes nothing even while creating. It is His nature. He alone is *caitanya ātman,* the conscious Self.

ज्ञानं बन्धः

jñānaṃ bandhaḥ

Knowledge is bondage.

Śiva Sūtra 1.2

Amazing as it is, this aphorism is completely true. Our inner states—contraction or expansion, joy or sorrow, anxiety or ignorance—are all reactions to outer stimuli. Knowledge of the external world is the root of all sorrow when it seeps inside and we identify with it.

When I was a child, I used to stroll through an area where English was spoken. Some of the boys there would taunt me in English. Since I didn't understand what they said, I would only laugh and go on my way. Then one day a person who spoke English explained to me that I was being ridiculed. As soon as I heard that, I was unhappy.

Outer knowledge causes bondage in exactly the same way. This is what Mahādev, Lord Śiva, says here. When we identify ourselves with the body and the status and titles that belong to it, then pride of family, caste, and individuality eclipse our inner nature, and there is bondage. Our concepts of sin and virtue and our identification with the gross and subtle bodies alienate us from our true Self. To go about life without interest in the Self and to mistake ignorance for knowledge is bondage, and that bondage is the cause of all misery.

When by the Guru's grace the inner Śakti is awakened, knowledge of the Self arises from within. The Self stands revealed. And when the Self and Brahman are seen to be one, a person lives in supreme freedom and relishes his own play. He revels in the freedom of supreme bliss. This great bliss becomes perfect Self-realization.

ज्ञानाधिष्ठानं मातृका

jñānādhiṣṭhānaṃ mātṛkā

Mātṛkā [the power of sound inherent in the letters of the alphabet] is the source of limited knowledge.

Śiva Sūtra 1.4

When Paraśakti—who is also called Citi Bhagavatī, the universal Consciousness—limits Herself, She manifests in the form of *mātṛkā*, the group of letters, or sound-syllables. *Mātṛkā* is the cause of one's pain and pleasure. All the thoughts and feelings that arise in the mind—happiness and unhappiness, desire, agitation, love, expectation, and jealousy—are the work of *mātṛkā*. Neither language, nor terminology, nor poetry, nor scriptures, nor words of praise and blame can pass beyond the world of letters.

Mātṛkā arises in the heart, from the inner speech. There are four levels of speech corresponding to the four bodies. Everyone is aware of the speech of the tongue. It is called *vaikharī* and corresponds to the gross body. With the subtle intellect, one can also know the second level of speech, which is in the throat. There, words have taken form but have not yet emerged. This level is called *madhyamā* and corresponds to the subtle body. At a deeper level, words exist in the heart. This is the third level of speech, *paśyantī*, which corresponds to the causal body. Here, words are hidden, and what arises at this level is *mātṛkā*. Beneath this level is a fourth level, *parā*, which corresponds to the supracausal body. Some say that *parā* is in the navel region, but in actuality this subtlest level of speech pervades everywhere. Since it is all-pervading, it can be known anywhere. *Mātṛkā* has its source in the *parā* level.

Letters combine to form a word—for example, *m-a-n-g-o* becomes *mango*. Each word has its own meaning, the meaning creates its own image, and that image has its own feeling.

Whenever an image is created in the mind, one experiences an emotion, whether it is happiness or unhappiness, friendship or enmity. For example, if I call someone a fool, the letters come together and compose words, the words compose a sentence, the sentence has its own meaning, and the meaning creates its own image. When I utter the sentence "That girl is a fool," it strikes her, and a painful and angry feeling arises in her mind.

Mātṛkā creates infinite images. If one doesn't identify with the images or their objects, one doesn't experience suffering.

Mātṛkā is the source not only of our pain and pleasure but of this entire universe. This world has arisen from the sound-syllables of the Sanskrit alphabet, which are nothing but *mātṛkā.* Just as it creates the outer world, *mātṛkā* creates infinite inner worlds. Different feelings arise in the heart, and the individual soul keeps moving among these feelings throughout its life, experiencing pain and pleasure. Day and night, the *mātṛkā śakti* creates these things within us. Even when we sleep, it doesn't sleep. It is alive even in the *savikalpa* state of *samādhi,* the *samādhi* with thought. It dies only when one attains the state of thoughtlessness, *nirvikalpa samādhi.*

Mātṛkā is the source of the three *malas,* the impurities that cause knowledge to become contracted. Due to *āṇavamala,* one feels imperfect; due to *māyīyamala,* one becomes lost in duality; and due to *kārmamala,* one becomes caught up in the fruit of one's good and bad actions. Instead of understanding that one is the Self, one understands oneself to be a mere human being. One feels "I am a man," "I am a priest," "I am a woman," "I am thin," and in this way, one makes oneself small. In the inner space, *mātṛkā śakti* creates letters and one experiences them. One begins to dwell in them, one becomes infatuated with them, and as a result, one performs actions in this world. This is worldliness.

However, just as *mātṛkā* helps us to contract, it also helps us to expand ourselves. The moment one understands the *mātṛkā śakti* and its work, one is no longer a human being. When the *mātṛkā śakti* expands within, in this very body one becomes Śiva.

Sit quietly and watch the play of the *mātṛkā śakti.* Watch how the *mātṛkā* gives rise to letters, how the letters compose words, how the meaning of the words creates images in the mind; watch how you become involved in these images.

The yogi pursues *mātṛkā śakti;* he watches it and makes it steady. He brings it under his control, he manipulates it any way he likes. He turns evil thoughts into good thoughts. The *mātṛkā śakti* works according to his will. Such a yogi is called a conqueror of the senses.

One who understands the play of *mātṛkā śakti* and makes it still rises above pain and pleasure. One cannot attain peace as long as he is driven by the play of the *mātṛkā śakti.* For this reason, one has to practice yoga. Through yoga, the movements of the mind are stilled and the power of *mātṛkā* is overcome.

उद्यमो भैरवः

udyamo bhairavaḥ

Effort is itself Bhairava.

Śiva Sūtra 1.5

The only true effort is this: on attaining knowledge of the nature of the highest reality, one strives to remain constantly immersed in the awareness of the inner Self.

When the Guru's grace is received, one's inner Śakti is unfolded. As a result of the transmission of Śakti, the power of Consciousness, meditation comes spontaneously, and innumerable *kriyās,* including *āsanas, mudrās,* and different kinds of *prāṇāyāma,* take place. The seeker turns within. Awareness of the inner Self begins to throb all the time within him. To stay in this awareness is the right effort for the seeker.

Limited knowledge relying on words produces only dualities such as love and hate, joy and sorrow. But the undifferentiated awareness of one's true nature, which is the same as Bhairava, Śiva, releases pure bliss. To remain aware of the inner Self is right effort. To understand that all thoughts are nothing but the pulsation of Paraśakti anchors one firmly in the Self.

When one who constantly dives into his inner being is blessed by the Guru, he is blessed with a complete inner unfolding. This is known as the *śāmbhava* way:

अकिञ्चित्चिन्तकस्यैव गुरुणा प्रतिबोधतः ।
जायते यः समावेश शाम्भवोऽसावुदीरितः ॥

akincitcintakasyaiva guruṇā pratibodhataḥ /
jāyate yaḥ samāveśaḥ śāmbhavo'sāvudīritaḥ //

[That *śāmbhava* state is described as the absorption of one in whom there is no thought. This arises in one who has been awakened by the Guru.]

Mālinīvijaya Tantra 2.23

Even if an aspirant hasn't done any sadhana before meeting his Guru, and even if he hasn't explored the spiritual world, as long as he has faith, he experiences unity with the supreme Lord once he is initiated by the Guru. The greater the maturity of a disciple, the higher his worth and sincerity, the quicker his progress toward merging in Śāmbhava, in Śiva. To achieve awareness of one's perfection through the *śāmbhavopāya,* through this approach—that alone is right effort. And right effort is itself Bhairava, the supreme Self.

जाग्रत्स्वप्नसुषुप्तभेदे तुर्याभोगसम्भवः

jāgratsvapnasuṣuptabhede turyābhogasambhavaḥ

[It is possible to] enjoy the bliss of *turīya* [the fourth, or transcendental, state] in the different states of waking, dream, and deep sleep.

Śiva Sūtra 1.7

This is a significant aphorism and worth contemplating. It hints at the high state of the *jñānī*, the fully enlightened being. Most people think that a *jñānī*, a saint, is someone who lives in silence, in a cave, his eyes closed, his breath and other functions suspended for long periods, lost in *samādhi*. But to a real *jñānī*, such a yogi is only a child. Having come to know the true nature of reality through his Guru's grace, a *jñānī* has ceased to differentiate the waking, dream, deep sleep, and *turīya* states from one another. To him each of them is equally full of the same supreme bliss. A *jñānī* would not condemn the waking state, nor would he avoid participation in its drama. Neither does he find anything wrong with the dream or deep sleep states.

A *jñānī's* attention is not on the passing states, but on the Witness-Self who, while living in those states, remains different from them, forever beyond their reach. The Self is detached, watching the waking state from a distance. Coming into contact with the senses and their objects, the Self remains separate from them. And even when acting in the waking state, the Self does not identify with the waking state, remaining its witness. While dreaming, when the body is asleep, the Self does not become identified with that state either, but sees the dream world as distinct from itself. Though it gets into the dream state, the Self remains as a spectator to all its happenings. And in the deep sleep state, the Self remains the detached observer. That Witness-Self is experienced in *turīya*.

In *turīya* one drinks the highest bliss. But a real *jñānī* or yogi, seeing the entire waking world as an expansion of the same Citi, drinks the ecstasy of *samādhi,* the bliss of manifestation, even in the waking state. He knows from direct experience that in all the states—one arising from the other, one merging into the other—the Witness-Self always remains undifferentiated, pure and unaffected, unchanged, without rising or setting. Such a *jñānī,* who is perfect in meditation, who has been blessed by his Guru, continually enjoys the same bliss of *turīya,* without the least change, in all the states—waking, dream, and deep sleep. Of course he is full of peace while he is meditating, but even while immersed in the affairs of the waking world, he is free of anxiety, always reveling in the bliss that surges from within. To that great soul, there is nothing to renounce, nothing to acquire, for there is nothing different from himself.

The bliss that is the same and unchanged in all the states is the bliss of *turīya.* To an actor, all the scenes in a play are equally his creation and his joyful sport; whether they provoke tears or laughter, they mean the same to him. In the same way, the three states—waking, dream, and deep sleep—are simply different phases of the same supreme state of *turīya.* The bliss of *turīya* can be enjoyed in all its purity in all the states.

ज्ञानं जाग्रत्

jñānaṃ jāgrat

Knowledge is wakefulness.

Śiva Sūtra 1.8

In reality, the normal waking state is not true wakefulness. According to enlightened sages, the state of waking, being coupled with ignorance, is darkness. The poet-saints of India exhort, "O friend, why are you asleep in the arms of ignorance? Wake up. Awake!" The Upaniṣads also cry, "Arise! Awake! Don't sleep!" Forgetfulness of one's true nature is ignorance, and that is a night of terrible darkness.

If a person's Kuṇḍalinī is asleep, he is wrapped in folds of night; he is not truly awake, not awake to the Self. It is only when, by the Guru's grace, the great Śakti Kuṇḍalinī awakes within him that a person emerges from sleep. One who sleeps is not aware of the magnificent kingdom of Citi within his own heart, nor of the true nature of the external world.

The awakening of Kuṇḍalinī is the dawn of knowledge. As soon as one receives the Guru's grace, the sleep of ignorance disappears, the inner eye of knowledge is opened. While sitting with the mind focused on the heart, one can know the inner and outer worlds with great clarity. One can see the Blue Lord (*nīleśvara*) in the *sahasrāra* sparkling with the effulgence of a million suns.[2] This is the light of inner knowledge, and it dispels the darkness of ignorance and reveals the entire inner universe.

Just as a drop of rain by merging with a river becomes the river, and a river by flowing into the ocean becomes the ocean itself, the embodied soul by merging with Paraśiva becomes Paraśiva Himself. The person whose eye of knowledge is opened becomes transmuted into pure Consciousness. In the great blue spaces of Consciousness, Citi sports and revels in Her fullness. By Her light, a person begins to shine like a diamond.

Only one who has evolved from the state of ignorance to the state of full knowledge is truly awake. Waves of the bliss of unity-awareness ripple through him. For him, there is neither one nor two nor many; neither matter nor Consciousness; neither *jīva* nor Śiva; neither gods nor goddesses. He melts the ice of name and form in the ocean of Consciousness, himself becoming pure Consciousness. He transcends both doing and becoming. He is pure Śiva. This is the pure awakening to knowledge received by the Guru's grace. It is the transcendental, supreme Śiva. It is Guru Nityananda.

त्रितयभोक्ता वीरेशः

tritayabhoktā vīreśaḥ

The supreme Lord
is the experiencer of the three states.

Śiva Sūtra 1.11

The yogi who has become one with universal Consciousness is centered in the supreme state of Śiva and, like Śiva, experiences himself as the witness of the three states and the three worlds.

The Self, who is the witness of the waking, dream, and deep sleep states, is indeed Śiva, the supreme Lord. As witness, He enjoys these states without undergoing any change. In the waking state, He functions in the gross body and experiences gross objects with the five organs of perception, the five organs of action, the five forms of *prāṇa*, and the fourfold psychic instrument.[3] In dreams, He experiences the subtle pleasures of that state. And in deep sleep, He experiences joyful and dreamless oblivion.

Supreme Śiva is the real experiencer of all the states. As the Lord says in the *Bhagavadgītā*, it is He who enjoys and digests the four kinds of food by becoming the gastric fire, *vaiśvānara*. In their delusion, people think, "I am the one experiencing . . . I am the one who is doing . . ." This attitude is bondage. Who but Śiva can hear through the ears? Who but Śiva can think with the mind and speak with the tongue? The *Bhagavadgītā* says:

सर्वेन्द्रियगुणाभासम्

sarvendriyaguṇābhāsam

He is the perceiver of all sense objects. [3.15]

Who but Śiva can perceive sense objects? The One who experiences the external waking world, the internal world of dreams, and the total oblivion of deep sleep is the supreme Lord of *turīya*. By remaining constantly aware of the witness of the three states and their phenomena, a seeker finds the place of *turīya,* and even beyond, right within himself.

Both the seer and the seen are the same supreme Consciousness. The relationship of the senses and the sense objects is this: while the senses perceive, delight in, and act on their respective objects, Śiva is the experience and Śiva is what is experienced. One who plunges into the inner Self with this knowledge and with a still mind becomes God.

विस्मयो योगभूमिकाः

vismayo yogabhūmikāḥ

Yogic realizations are amazing.

Śiva Sūtra 1.12

The yogi is filled with amazement by the realizations he attains as the Guru's grace unfolds itself. A person may naturally feel surprised by unusual things in ordinary life, but nothing in the outer world can compare to yogic realizations. When his inner Śakti is awakened by the grace of the Guru, the yogi starts having marvelous inner experiences. Countless physical and subtle *kriyās* take place within him spontaneously. Sitting in one place, he sees distant objects and many different worlds. He enters the space of the heart, and there he sees the worlds of meditation, *tandra* and *vidyā*. He roams in the white and blue and gold effulgence of the inner spaces. He envisions the heart seed. He moves into the *sahasrāra* and sees its radiant sphere. Every day there are new wonders that fill him with amazement and great rapture.

He continues to pursue yogic practice and to explore his own nature, experiencing ever-new *kriyās*. And when the bliss of the Self arises from within, he is surprised, amazed, and completely stilled.

By means of the Guru's grace, the yogi perceives that the cosmos exists within himself. He is astonished by visions of all the gods and goddesses and the various *śaktis* within his own being, and in time he becomes aware of his unity with the entire universe. Then, immersed in the awareness of inner blue radiance, he unceasingly sees himself in all, and all in himself. He is submerged in the blissful ocean of amazement.

इच्छाशक्तिर् उमा कुमारी

icchāśaktir umā kumārī

The power of will is the maiden Umā.

Śiva Sūtra 1.13

God, called the Puruṣa in the Upaniṣads, is the final goal of all philosophical systems. In His being a vibration arises spontaneously. This is His power of will, and it is in no way different from Him. In the word *kumārī*, the syllable *ku* is *māyā*, the power that gives rise to the awareness of differences; *mārī* is that which destroys. *Umā kumārī* is the maiden who dissolves the consciousness of differences.

The maiden, Umā, this power of will, creates an independent universe within Her own being. She creates this richly diverse universe of dualities and contradictions: it is different from Her and yet not different. Though She Herself becomes the universe, She remains exactly what She has always been: a maiden, ever youthful.

She arises in the central channel (*suṣumṇā nāḍī*) of a seeker who has received the grace of the Guru. She carries out various functions, purifying every single part of the seeker's being, performing yogic *kriyās* as they are needed. In the end, She unites with supreme Śiva in the *sahasrāra* and manifests Herself fully. It is then that the yogi attains the highest freedom.

A Siddha is one who, merging with the divine will, has become utterly free and lives and moves everywhere without the least hindrance. For such a Master of yoga—who sees nothing as different from himself, who is capable of entering any realm with total ease and freedom—his will is the maiden Umā. It is truly She who is the universe.

शुद्धतत्त्वसन्धानाद् वा अपशुशक्तिः

śuddhatattvasandhānād vā apaśuśaktiḥ

By the awareness of pure being,
unbounded divine power is attained.

Śiva Sūtra 1.16

Paraśiva, the primordial Lord, the Guru of all Siddhas, is Himself supremely pure being. To worship Paraśiva knowing that you yourself are Paraśiva is to worship pure being. By this practice, a seeker rids himself of the fetters that bind him.

Śrī Jñāneśvar Mahāraj says in his *Jñāneśvarī* that just as a person can see a pot as clay without having to break it to pieces, in the same way, one should cultivate the awareness of the Self as the universe without discarding the universe or running away from it. This is the awareness of pure being, and by its means one easily attains the state of the Lord, the Master of the world.

One who wishes to meditate on pure being should meditate on Paraśiva, who equally pervades everywhere, within and without. Meditate on the external universe, considering every bit of it—animate and inanimate—as pure Consciousness. Not only the supremely effulgent Consciousness within one's heart, but also the senses and the body are the same Citi. Regarding all aspects of the world this way, with a mind free from thought, one rises above the state of bondage and merges into supreme light. The scriptures say:

सर्वदेहचिन्मयं हि जगद्वा परिभावयेत् ।
युगपन्निर्विकल्पेन मनसा परमोद्भवः ॥

sarvadehacinmayaṃ hi jagadvā paribhāvayet /
yugapannirvikalpena manasā paramodbhavaḥ //

[It consists of the Consciousness in all bodies
and contains the entire world, and at the same time,
it is the supreme source of a mind that is free from thought.]

Here the aspirant is asked to meditate with a silent mind. If he could look upon the unceasing flow of images that arise in his mind as nothing but the mind, he would be free. In the same way that the universe made of Consciousness is Consciousness, and pots made from clay are clay, and ornaments beaten out of gold are still gold, and cloth woven from thread is thread, so that phantasmagoria of innumerable thoughts and fancies is nothing but the mind. And the mind is throbbing Citi. By this true insight, the mind becomes tranquil. To become perfectly still, seeing the whole cosmos as a play of Consciousness and submerging oneself in that divine play, to meditate on Śiva by becoming Śiva—this is the awareness of pure being.

वितर्क आत्मज्ञानम्

vitarka ātmajñānam

Right understanding is knowledge of the Self.

Śiva Sūtra 1.17

"I am the same Paraśiva who becomes the universe and dwells in its heart"—when this thought, uninterrupted by doubt, vibrates within, one has attained right understanding (*vitarka*), knowledge of the inner Self.

After the compassionate transmission of Śakti by the Guru, impurities are washed away by yogic *kriyās* and pure knowledge wells up: the seeker becomes constantly possessed by the awareness of the inner Self and the experience of the supreme Śakti. By regular, daily meditation, the process is aided; the subtle inner *kriyās* remove all taints from the heart. This happens easily with the Guru's unwavering love. The primordial Guru calls that knowledge *vitarka* when it arises from the heart as a perception of the essential unity of the world's apparently diverse forms. The body, the *prāṇa,* and the senses may appear distinct from one another, but they are one with Consciousness.

With the help of the Guru's teachings, one must have firm faith that God alone has become the universe as both *krama* and *akrama. Krama* is God as the graded, systematic universe in form. *Akrama* is God pervading everything everywhere, equally, at all times. Paraśiva, the supreme Self, has Himself assumed countless forms and diversities in a graded succession (*krama*). At the same time He maintains His nonhierarchical, nonsuccessive (*akrama*) character. In His essential nature, He remains ever the same, in primal omniscience and omnipotence, completely, eternally perfect. To have perfect understanding is *vitarka.* It is this awareness: "I am the same Paraśiva who is the One, the Self of all."

लोकानन्दः समाधिसुखम्

lokānandaḥ samādhisukham

The bliss of *loka* is the bliss of *samādhi.*

Śiva Sūtra 1.18

Loka includes the whole multitude of things that can be perceived by the inner and outer senses. In this context, all things that can be known, together with the beings who know them, are called *loka.* This is the yogi's understanding of the terms *perceiver* and *perceived*: by the yoga of knowledge, he comes to realize that the seer is the seen and the seen is the seer. Normally when two people are looking at each other, each appears as the object of perception to the other. But to the *jñānī,* the perceiver is also the object of perception. Such awareness allows him to rest in the realization of the knowledge "I am Śiva." This is supreme bliss. This is the highest *samādhi,* the ultimate state of enlightenment. The yogi who looks upon the universe as his own body drinks the nectar of ecstasy. He sees the vast variety of forms—everything animate and inanimate, the endless modifications around him—as diverse and yet one, for they all appear in his own indivisible Self. For him all worlds are vibrations of the one Self, throbbing with its bliss. This is the bliss of *loka,* the ecstasy of *samādhi.*

Such a one does not have to retire to a cave or a desolate forest. He does not have to force his eyes to remain closed or suspend his breath to pass into an inert *samādhi.* He is always in the natural state of *samādhi,* while eating, drinking, sleeping, waking, playing, talking, bathing, enjoying sense pleasures, and meditating. He always lives in spontaneous joy.

This is the bliss of *loka,* the ecstasy of *samādhi.*

शुद्धविद्योदयाच्चक्रेशत्वसिद्धिः

śuddhavidyodayāccakreśatvasiddhiḥ

When pure knowledge arises, lordship over all cosmic power is attained.

Śiva Sūtra 1.21

Knowledge is of two types: pure and impure. If you think, "I am a sinner, I am a limited being"; if you suffer from a poverty of Śakti; if you are obsessed with others' faults and evil in the world; to the degree that you take on those tendencies, you are under the influence of impure knowledge.

Pure knowledge arises when the Guru's blessing sets you on the path of Siddha Yoga. The grace of the Guru purifies the inner being through yogic *kriyās,* inner light begins to glow, and the inner Self is revealed with the awareness "I am the One." This awareness gives rise to pure knowledge. Then one identifies oneself with the whole cosmos, feeling, "I am indeed everything; I alone pervade everywhere, within and without." This is mastery over the cosmic power. It is called *mahāmahaiśvarya,* the highest state of supreme Lordship.

One of pure knowledge understands that his essential nature is Śakti, operating of Her own free will; he sees himself as the embodiment of Paraśiva; and he discards the illusion "I am not Śiva." When he can hold these truths as a single perception, effortlessly and unceasingly, he is in the state of *vidyā* (knowledge). In this state, which is also called *unmanī* (that which transcends the mind), one's inner Self stands fully revealed.

Śivahood, the divine state, is perfect awareness of the inner Self and the realization that you yourself are Śiva, the supreme cause of everything, in His fullness. A Siddha is one who is established in this state. He has achieved perfect union with that Paraśiva who abides in the boundless space within the *sahasrāra.* Birth, death, poverty, and sorrow have no access here. One's identity with Śiva is the only awareness. It is a state beyond comprehension.

महाह्रदानुसन्धानान् मन्त्रवीर्यानुभवः

mahāhradānusandhānān mantravīryānubhavaḥ

By awareness of the great ocean, the potency of mantra is realized.

Śiva Sūtra 1.22

Paraśakti is universal Consciousness. By the power of Her own sweet will, She manifests all the gross sense objects from Her own being. This is the experience of those yogis who are unwavering and ceaseless in their identity with the Supreme. They also gain direct knowledge of certain dynamic forms of Śakti, who is known in different spheres by different names. When She moves in the inner sky of Consciousness, She is called Khecarī. When She moves through the fourfold inner psychic instrument, She is known as Gocarī. When She moves in different directions [through the sense organs], She is Dikcarī. And when She moves on the Earth [creating various objects], She is known as Bhūcarī.

Paraśakti remains absolutely pure and detached, reflecting the whole universe in Herself just as a mirror reflects an image. Though She is manifest in the world around us, Her mystery is difficult to comprehend. That is why She is also called the great ocean, the unfathomable ocean. Just as an ocean may be tranquil even while holding rocks, mountains, trees, and gigantic creatures in its depths, so the Goddess Saṃvitti (universal Consciousness) remains serene while holding the cosmos within Herself. One who carries on his spiritual practice with this awareness experiences the potency of mantra (*mantravīrya*). The direct experience of Paraśakti as universal Consciousness, the dawning of perfect bliss in the heart—this is the realization of the power of mantra.

चित्तं मन्त्रः

cittaṃ mantraḥ

The mind is mantra.

Śiva Sūtra 2.1

This is a key aphorism; it can be the foundation for a sadhana of liberation. Virtually all religions—including Hinduism, Islam, Zoroastrianism, Judaism, and Christianity--practice their own forms of mantra repetition. Though we have much reverence for mantras and faith in them, we find that we do not gain as much from them as we expect. On the contrary, we remain in misery. It is because we are ignorant of the true potency of mantra that the mantra deity does not manifest.

In this aphorism Paraśiva gives us the secret of mantra: the mind of the aspirant who practices mantra is itself the mantra. By means of the mind we become aware of the supreme truth. It is with this mind that we repeat mantras, we contemplate their meaning, we come to know their essence and their goal.

When we hear the name Rāma, it is our mind that relates it to a particular entity by our understanding of the two Sanskrit syllables *rā* and *ma*. It is also with our mind that we understand the meaning of the sacred syllable *Oṃ*. The scriptures say:

ॐ इत्येकाक्षरं ब्रह्मन् ॐ जगत् ॐ सर्वम्

Oṃ ityekākṣaraṃ brahman Oṃ jagat Oṃ sarvam

Oṃ is Brahman in the form of one syllable.
Oṃ is the universe. *Oṃ* is all.

This one pulsation is the throb underlying the entire universe. Our understanding of the highest reality is based on our comprehension of this single syllable, *Oṃ*. *Oṃ* is the symbol for the pulsation of the highest *tattvas,* the highest levels of creation.

In the same way, we must consider mantra to be one with the supreme Self. Mantra is the undifferentiated, integral awareness of the nature of the Divine; it should not be regarded as separate from God. Being one with God, it is full of bliss. It arises by itself. It is the vibration of mantra that springs forth as a universe. The whole cosmos throbs in the mind, which is itself mantra. The person who attains oneness with mantra by remaining in unity-consciousness annihilates the world of dualities. This is why for the person who repeats it, a mantra is the protector, the supreme means, the highest deity.

मननात् त्रायते इति मन्त्रः

mananāt trāyate iti mantraḥ

Mantra is that which protects and redeems
one who contemplates it.

One who constantly repeats a mantra with correct understanding is raised by its power to divinity. This is the purpose of mantra. In the scriptures, it is said that mantra transforms the one who repeats it into the Lord's own form.

It is important to see that we are not primarily concerned with the component syllables of a mantra or its deity in the usual sense. Here the word *mantra* refers to the mind, particularly to the throbbing movement of the mind by which a yogi meditates. Syllables uttered aloud do not constitute a mantra. Indeed, mantra is the great Śakti who brings the syllables to life; it is the awareness of inner unity.

The mantra loses its power if the mantra, the repeater, and the supreme Lord who is the goal of the mantra are kept in three separate compartments. The mantra will never bring realization that way. The distinction between an object and its name is imaginary. If a seeker distinguishes between the worshiper and the worshiped, the devotee and the Lord, he can never achieve realization:

पृथङ् मन्त्रः पृथङ् मन्त्री न सिद्धयति कदाचन

pṛthaṅ mantraḥ pṛthaṅ mantrī na siddhayati kadācana

The mantra syllables, the mantra deity,
and the mantra repeater form an indistinguishable unity.

This is the truth. They appear to be different only to an intellect caught in dualities. Paraśiva is the cause of the universe; from Him alone the entire gross and subtle cosmos comes. His Śakti, Citi, creates the world for Her sport, holds it in Her own being, and gathers it up into Herself. Thus the various deities, innumerable mantras, rules and rituals, time and space are all nothing but universal Consciousness. The Consciousness of unity pulsing within a seeker is mantra. The one who repeats the mantra is Śiva, the mantra *Namaḥ Śivāya* is Śiva, and the Lord of the mantra—its goal—is Śiva. The secret of the realization of a mantra lies in repeating it, having identified oneself completely with Śiva. In the *Svacchanda Tantra,* Lord Śiva says:

आत्मनो भैरवं रूपं भावयेद् यस् तु पुरुषः ।
तस्य मन्त्रः प्रसिद्ध्यति नित्ययुक्तस्य सुन्दरि ।।

ātmano bhairavaṃ rupaṃ bhāvayed yas tu puruṣaḥ /
tasya mantraḥ prasiddhyati nityayuktasya sundari //

O Goddess, only he who knows that Śiva is within himself
as himself realizes the goal of the mantra. [I.137]

प्रयत्नः साधकः

prayatnaḥ sādhakaḥ

A seeker is one who makes an effort.

Śiva Sūtra 2.2

This is the second aphorism of *śāktopāya* [the second section of the *Śiva Sūtra* and the means to Self-realization through use of the mind]. In the preceding *sūtra,* the nature, power, and qualities of mantra were explained by equating mantra with the mind. The present aphorism is speaking of a yogi who is constantly contemplating his mantra. The practice that joins God and aspirant into an inviolable unity is here called "effort." The sadhana by which a seeker who has been wandering in a state of spiritual bondage becomes anchored in his true nature upon receiving the Guru's grace, like an arrow hitting its target—this is "effort" as revealed by the Guru. The constant awareness of the supreme mantra, which is vibrating Citi, is right effort. *Effort* here does not have its usual meaning of repeating particular mantras in a particular manner; in a particular place; using the teeth, lips, tongue, and vocal cords in a particular way to produce a particular sound. Right effort is quite a different thing; it involves the complete identification of the meditating seeker with the object of meditation.

Lord Śiva says that only he receives the fruit of mantra who is constantly making right effort. A mantra becomes *caitanya*—it comes to life—by a seeker's effort. A mantra has come alive when, by the Guru's grace, Kuṇḍalinī is activated and the supreme Self—which manifests as inner lights and inner *kriyās*—is the aim of mantra repetition. The seeker becomes aware of the oneness of the mantra, its practicer, and its deity constantly—in meditation, in worldly dealings, and in all sense activities. The exhalation and inhalation become the component syllables of the mantra. Another way of saying this is that the outbreath and inbreath are combined with the great mantra received from the Guru, which is repeated with unity-awareness. This is the effort a seeker makes.

Paraśiva, the supreme Self, is the deadly enemy of duality and differentiation. As the greatest advocate of nonduality, He has become the Self of all, the means that sustains all bodies. He has become the universe composed of twenty-five *tattvas.*[4] Food and water are His manifestations as well as knowledge, devotion, and yoga. The highest effort consists of attaining nondual devotion for Him, in the awareness "I am Śiva."

Śivena śivasādhanaḥ. "Śiva is realized by means of Śiva." Therefore, you should discard concepts such as "world," "bound soul," and "evil thoughts" and practice identification with Śiva. Live in the awareness of your Śivahood, your divinity. You are Śiva's. Become Śiva and nothing but Śiva.

विद्यासमुत्थाने स्वाभाविके खेचरी शिवावस्था

vidyāsamutthāne svābhāvike khecarī śivāvasthā

When pure knowledge arises,
khecarī, the state of Śiva, is easily attained.

Śiva Sūtra 2.5

Pure, supreme knowledge arises in a seeker blessed by the grace of the Guru, and he is filled with discrimination and right understanding. He loses all interest in trivial *siddhis* and is absorbed in his natural state, bliss-consciousness. He becomes permanently established in the sky of pure awareness, where there is only bliss. This is *khecarī. Khe* (or *kha*) is the sky of pure awareness, the space of Consciousness. *Carī* is one who moves, delights, or soars in that sky; one who hears the melodies of the space of Consciousness and enjoys the bliss that bubbles up from within. So *khecarī* is known as the state of Śiva.

On receiving the Guru's grace, a seeker should sit firmly in a meditative posture. One should focus the mind on the *maṇipūra cakra, anāhata cakra, ājñā cakra,* or *sahasrāra*. One should merge all the senses into the Self and become completely absorbed in it. One should meditate on Śiva, seeing Him in every thought and object, and lose oneself in this meditation. Thus the seeker will realize Brahman.

In meditation the world of illusory differences, the arena of all our sorrow and restlessness, is dissolved in unity-consciousness. The universe is assimilated into the Self in blissful union, and the power of mantra is realized. When the mantra, which is Citi, or the great Consciousness, becomes pleased with a yogi, it imparts all its potency to him. As long as the power of mantra is not manifested, it is a barren mantra. When the inner Śakti awakens, *kriyāyoga* begins to work and one passes into meditation; the awareness "I am Śiva" dawns. As this awareness becomes constant, the power of mantra is fully gained. It flows from identification with Śiva.

Mudrā or *khecarī mudrā* refers to the highest state, the state of supreme Bhairava or Śiva. The everlasting peace of Śiva comes to that seeker who enters the *khecarī* state and is awakened by the Guru's knowledge. He is a *mahāyogī*. Forever dwelling in the sky of Consciousness he is called Paraśiva.

गुरुर् उपायः

gurur upāyaḥ

The Guru is the means.

Śiva Sūtra 2.6

For absorption in the supreme Self, the Guru is the most effective means. Even Lord Śiva agrees that a disciple's Self-unfolding takes place only by the grace of the Guru. The Guru destroys the darkness in the hearts of his disciples and fills them with the light of knowledge.

The Guru is one who dispenses divine power. The Guru should not be confused with a particular physical form, nor does a flair for scholarship or literary talent make one a Guru. The Guru is one in whom the divine power of grace has taken permanent abode.

Even an ordinary teacher can impart a mantra, prescribe a technique, or explain the scriptures. He alone is the supreme Guru who enters his disciple as grace, blessing him with shaktipat and transforming him into the Guru, like himself. The Guru who reveals the potency of mantra in a disciple is unquestionably himself Śiva. It is by the power of mantra that the Kuṇḍalinī wakes, inner yoga is initiated, and the highest truth, the supreme Lord, is directly experienced. Such a Guru, the most effective of means for his disciples, is truly hard to find.

शरीरं हविः

śarīraṃ haviḥ

The body is the offering.

Śiva Sūtra 2.8

Many modes of worship by sacrifice have been prevalent in the world since the time of the Vedas. In all these rituals, certain materials are used as offerings. The performer, or the sacrificer, makes herbal offerings to the fire while reciting mantras. Here Lord Śiva says that a yogi does not perform such sacrifices. A yogi obtains *mahāyoga* by Guru's grace and offers his own body to the divine fire of Kuṇḍalinī. He offers his individuality as an oblation to the fire of knowledge, and then the fire of yoga blazes within him. Such a lord of yoga offers the entire cosmos to the fire of Consciousness through knowledge. By Guru's grace, his Śakti is activated, and *mahāyoga* begins its work within him. His body is purged through yoga, his eye of knowledge opens, and he sees the true nature of the universe. The diversities of the world are consumed in the fire of knowledge, the light of the Self, and all that remains is the play of universal Consciousness.

Such a yogi is not bound by what others consider to be chains: sin, sorrow, and agitation do not grieve him. He does not feel hostile to enemies nor attached to friends. A yogi who has offered his body to the fire of Consciousness, wherever he may be—in heaven or in our mortal world—considers everything to be Consciousness. He submits all distinctions, sins, and sorrows to the purifying fire of yoga and becomes one with Śiva.

शिवोऽस्मि साधनाविष्टः

śivo'smi sādhanāviṣṭaḥ

I am Śiva—with this thought
one surrenders oneself to sadhana.

Śivadṛṣṭi 7.98

Identification with Śiva is his sadhana. To him,

शिवो भोक्ता शिवो भोज्य शिवो कर्ता शिवः
कर्मः शिवो करणात्मकः

śivo bhoktā śivo bhojya śivo kartā śivaḥ
karmaḥ śivo karaṇātmakaḥ

Śiva is the experiencer and the object of experience.
Śiva is the goal of sadhana.
Śiva is the sacrifice and the materials used in the sacrifice.
Śiva is the sacrificer and the ritual as well.
Śiva is all the sense organs and the mind.

The yogi surrenders his world with all its dualities and himself as well to Paraśiva.

Paraśiva says, "The body is the offering." A yogi is one who consumes his gross and subtle bodies in the fire of Consciousness, consumes the outer universe also in the same fire, and lives in identity with Śiva. On completing his sadhana, on attaining perfection, he is immersed in supreme bliss. That is his ritualistic, sacrificial bath.

ज्ञानम् अन्नम्

jñānam annam

Knowledge is food.

Śiva Sūtra 2.9

Food is the very life of the embodied soul. By food the body arises; by food it is sustained; into food it merges in the end—the Earth is rich with food. The food that is nourishing to a yogi and brings him satisfaction and bliss is the awareness of his own nature, contented rest in his own *ātman*. In *sūtra* 1.2, knowledge was said to be bondage. That was outer knowledge, implying forgetfulness of one's nature and the presence of the ego-sense, the sense of "I" and "mine."

Knowledge becomes food when it is the knowledge of unity, arising by the grace of the Guru. This knowledge transcends the imaginary distinctions of logic: matter and consciousness, one Soul and many souls, the individual and the universal, the atom and the cosmos, bondage and liberation. This knowledge takes one beyond the reach of death, time, and limitation to the supreme Self and supreme contentment. Knowledge, then, is food in the sense that it gives perfect satisfaction and perfect rest.

The state of enlightenment devours the illusory differences that previously obsessed the yogi—concepts of death and life, matter and consciousness, creature and creator, body and soul, man and woman, the householder and the renunciant. Ignorance, too, is the food of a yogi.

By the inner understanding born of Guru's grace, the yogi devours both the merely conceptual knowledge that obstructs complete rest in the Self and the ignorance that hides his own spirit from him. He is then immersed in perfect inner contentment.

मोहावरणात् सिद्धिः

mohāvaraṇāt siddhiḥ

By the conquest of delusion
the supreme realization is attained.

Śiva Sūtra 3.6

Māyā deludes men; she is the great enchantress. She lives with everyone, merges with and manipulates everyone, and catches everyone in her snares. In the *Bhagavadgītā* the Lord says: *mama māyā duratyayā,* "My Māyā is hard to cross."

Her way of seeing is perverse—the real seems unreal, consciousness becomes matter. She makes God man, Śiva *jīva,* and the One many. Māyā gives rise to *āvaraṇa,* the veil. By meditation, by Guru's grace, the different *tattvas* can be experienced in their different forms. Yoga and various spiritual practices cannot reveal the supreme reality: only meditation can help realize it. The supreme *tattva* is always manifest, always perfect. Meditation removes the veil covering the light of the highest reality.

Paraśiva is without birth and death, without beginning and end. He is devoid of thought, He is self-evident and fills everything. The transcendent being exists everywhere, but in our delusion, we do not understand this. As our ignorance is destroyed, victory over the breath (*udāna jaya*) arises, unfolding the power of knowledge. This restraint of the breath, which is shaktipat, takes one beyond the outbreath and inbreath. The path leaves behind the gross aspect of breath and moves along the ladder of its most subtle aspect to the realization of the highest truth. The state of centeredness from which there is no return is *prāṇāyāma* (control of the breath).

The mind experiences sound, touch, form, taste, and smell. *Pratyāhāra* (withdrawal of the senses) is the focusing on the supreme truth, transcending the mind. To transcend *sattva, rajas,* and *tamas*[5] and know that Śiva can be experienced—

this is real *dhyāna* (meditation). "Supreme Śiva is within me always"—this awareness is *dhāraṇā* (concentration). The Śiva principle equally pervades the entire universe, including both subject and object. "I am not apart from Śiva"—to continually experience this is *samādhi,* the merging in highest reality.

नर्तकात्मा

nartakātmā

The Self is the dancer.

Śiva Sūtra 3.9

The God of the Self is quite appropriately called a dancer or a great actor. Supremely free, perfect light, He bestows His grace on everyone while concealing His true nature and enacting the states of waking, dream, and deep sleep within His own being. He is the Self because, in conscious sport, He manifests from Himself the wonderful drama of the deluding and binding occupations of the waking state, the strange worlds of the dream state, and the great void of deep sleep.

Who but Śiva can express the character of all beings and existence? Who but He has the power to project the drama of the three worlds? Paraśiva alone is the author and the director of the scenes in His universe. In the theater, the costumes; the speeches, gestures, and actions of the characters; the scenes of laughter and of tears; the hero Rāma and the villain Rāvaṇa—all are creations of the playwright. In the same way, all the moving and unmoving, sentient and insentient creatures comprise the varied dance of the Self. With true knowledge one sees that the God of the *ātman* is always enacting sportful scenes on His own stage, for His own delight and ecstasy.

रङ्गोऽन्तरात्मा

raṅgo'ntarātmā

The inner Self is the stage.

Śiva Sūtra 3.10

There is great mystery in this *sūtra.* The *ātman* manifests countless dramas in His nonbeing. He Himself becomes the stage, the actor, and the costumes. He enacts His dramas in Himself for His own sake and for His own delight.

The *ātman* who desires to manifest the drama of the universe is Himself the stage. The inner Self is the place where He enacts the scenes in which He wears strange and various costumes. He assumes limitations of His own will and enacts many plays. He never becomes empty.

Assuming physical bodies, He appears as separate entities. In this condition He manifests His mundane sport through the sense organs by means of His own dynamic Śakti. Becoming the subtle body, He transmigrates from one life-form to another in various births.

प्रेक्षकाणीन्द्रियाणि

prekṣakāṇīndriyāṇi

The senses are the spectators.

Śiva Sūtra 3.11

The senses are the spectators who watch the Self stage the drama of the universe in the theater of one's own being. The sport of the *ātman* is constantly observed by the five organs of perception, the five organs of action, and the fourfold psychic instrument. The king of yogis who has received the Guru's grace while watching the drama of the universe being rolled out attains Self-realization when he turns inward. His inner experience teaches him that the whole world springs from his own Self. His sense of differences dissolved, he rises to the awareness "I am Śiva."

धीवशात् सत्त्वसिद्धिः

dhīvaśāt sattvasiddhiḥ

The truth is realized by pure intellect.

Śiva Sūtra 3.12

As one sees that the expanding universe is the sport of the Self, the Exalted, there arises a divine awareness of the universe as an undifferentiated unity. This is steady, pure intellect surveying the nature of the Self. When the intellect becomes established in the conviction of the unity of all things, truth is realized. Then one can perceive even the subtlest throbbings of the Self.

The constant awareness that the universe is an unfolding of the one Self gives purity, universal love, refinement of intellect, and oneness with the Self.

सिद्धः स्वतन्त्रभावः

siddhaḥ svatantrabhāvaḥ

A Siddha lives in total freedom.

Śiva Sūtra 3.13

The state of a Siddha is the state of freedom.

For the embodied soul there are only two possibilities. One is the state of bondage in which he loses the awareness of his nature, his glory, his power of understanding, and becomes contracted. He feels, "I am small, I am a sinner, I am subject to birth and death." His own outlook is the thing that shrinks him day by day. As he meditates on and ponders his own limitations, he becomes completely bound.

The other possibility is the state of absolute freedom. By the grace of the Guru, a person's inner Śakti is awakened through the process of shaktipat. Unfolding, his Śakti fills him with consciousness, and he gradually is freed from cravings and desires, the pull of the sense organs, and from all limited states. He achieves total union with the supreme Self.

A person who has achieved mastery over his senses and their objects is called a Siddha. One who sees this world, which the ignorant experience as full of sorrow, to be the outer sport of Paraśakti is a Siddha. One who has risen above the three bodies and their corresponding states is a Siddha. One who has rid himself of notions of acceptance and rejection and has burned away the imaginary distinctions of virtue and sin, enjoyment and liberation, worldliness and spirituality in the fire of inner knowledge is a Siddha. That great soul regards all the thoughts that arise within him, whether good or bad, as the stirrings of the Self. One who has become the universe, the Lord of the universe, and the Soul of the universe; one who is his own path and his own destination; one who is fully active and yet supremely inactive; one who is aware "I am Śiva"—he is a Siddha.

यथा तत्र तथाऽन्यत्र

yathā tatra tathā'nyatra

As here, so elsewhere.

Śiva Sūtra 3.14

A Siddha, having attained supreme freedom, lives wholly in the Self. Faithfully following the path shown by his Guru, a yogi becomes emancipated from the cravings of his body, mind, and senses. He beholds the same light within and without, permeating his gross and subtle bodies: the light of his soul spreads through the whole universe. He discovers that all countries, all external worlds, all realms, and in fact the entire cosmos possess the same reality that is within him.

Here is the body, *prāṇa,* senses, and mind. *Elsewhere* is the outer universe. All things and all beings embody the same impalpable essence.

Drunk with the ecstasy of divine revelation, one devotee exclaims, "In the mirror of my heart there is the image of Mohammed, the Lord. Wherever I bow my head, I see His face. How glorious is the light that is Mohammed, the light created by God!" This is the perfection of truth. "Know that there is only one within and without—this is the Guru's teaching." This declaration from Guru Nanak is the revelation of a Siddha Master.

Greed, pleasure seeking, and sensuality are marks of the soul bound by duality; one who is free cannot be allured by any temptation of the world. Nondual-consciousness, awareness of the Self of all, is entirely beyond the reach and pull of the senses. To regard everything as one's own Self—this is perfect self-control and perfect freedom from desire.

आसनस्थः सुखं ह्रदे निमज्जति

āsanasthaḥ sukhaṃ hrade nimajjati

The yogi who is established in a steady posture
easily becomes immersed in the ocean [of the heart].

Śiva Sūtra 3.16

Here the word *āsana* does not mean a sitting posture, like *padmāsana* or *siddhāsana*; it means the posture of true knowledge and understanding. Constant awareness of the identity of the universe and the Self, of the all-pervading one being, is the steady posture. Remaining firm in this posture, one need not resort to other practices. He is continually reflecting, "I am Consciousness, which is both immanent and transcendent." The yogis who are steady in this contemplation rise above limited body-consciousness, shedding all their *saṃskāras,* their past impressions, and becoming absorbed in the bliss of the Self. They are easily immersed in that ocean of nectar from which the universe flows.

Those who have assumed this steady posture have no need to practice concentration, fixing their gaze above, below, or in the middle; in front or behind; right or left; on higher or lower centers; inside or outside the body. They don't have to turn their minds to some object of meditation. They don't have to meditate on the senses or primal elements. Dissolving all duality in unity with the Self and remaining in that condition is the state of liberation known as *nirābhāsa,* without appearance, without image. Such a state is possible only as a result of the Guru's initiation, which awakens the inner Śakti and stabilizes the mind in the heart, that vast ocean of bliss, the scene of Paraśakti's joyful reveling.

Devotion to the Guru enables the yogi to enter there. The yogi of steady posture finds his entrance through meditation, and when he comes out from his immersion in this ocean of the heart, he sees the sport of Paraśakti in the outer universe too. His natural meditation goes on whether he is seated or standing, conversing or performing sense functions. He beholds the bliss of his heart flowing all around him. This constant meditation comes only through the Guru's grace.

मग्नः स्वचित्तेन प्रविशेत्

magnaḥ svacittena praviśet

Becoming absorbed,
one should enter the inner mind.

Śiva Sūtra 3.21

By a subtle mental effort, one merges all states of mind into the Self. This is the state of the absorbed mind. Let the meditator enter the *suṣumṇā,* the subtle central channel, by means of the inner yoga obtained by Guru's grace. Let him discard all gross techniques like the inhalation, retention, and exhalation of the breath that constitute *prāṇāyāma.* The *prāṇa* entering the *suṣumṇā* by Kuṇḍalinī's favor begins to throb subtly. This is *mahāyoga.*

Prāṇāyāma, concentration, and meditation are physical means. A yogi who has received grace does not have to practice these. He should strive earnestly to become absorbed in the awareness "I am That." It is pure Consciousness. The inner *prāṇāyāma* occurring spontaneously in the *suṣumṇā* is the means by which this state can be entered. In this *sūtra,* "becoming absorbed" and entering "the inner mind" refer to the awareness of one's inner nature, or steady *So'ham* awareness.

प्राणसमाचारे समदर्शनम्

prāṇasamācāre samadarśanam

Evenness of breath brings equality-consciousness.

Śiva Sūtra 3.22

The breath is the most important thing in the body; it keeps the body alive. Without breath, without *prāṇa,* even the individual soul has no force. There is no consciousness without *prāṇa.* All beings, sentient or insentient, owe their existence to *prāṇa.*

When the *prāṇa* becomes uneven, the sense of duality arises and the mind weaves new webs of fancy. With thoughts and fancies arising, with the world of imagination continually appearing and disappearing, how can peace be in the mind? So a yogi strives to control his breath in order to control his mind. For this purpose, he resorts to a variety of yogic processes like *prāṇāyāma.*

As long as the exhalation and the inhalation are not equal, as long as they do not become balanced, there is no release from duality and no peace. When the inner Śakti awakes by Guru's grace, *prāṇa* is purified and becomes even, and unity-awareness arises. The recipient of the grace of the Guru experiences the throb of Paraśakti and experiences perfection in *śāktopāya.* The outbreath and inbreath become equal, and then awareness and matter, subtle and gross, are seen to be one, even as a person sees the different parts of his body as one. The awareness of the equality of all things dawns: the mantra, its component syllables, the Guru, the mantra deity, and the mantra repeater are indeed perceived to be one. Then the yogi sees that the whole universe lives by the support of his inner Self. He sees the same mass of bliss-consciousness moving in all names and forms, and in all the outward-oriented thoughts of his mind.

Such a yogi lives in the divine state of unity with Śiva under all conditions of life. He sees that the one being pervades all castes and races, all stages of life, all deities, all materials and objects, all facets of worldly existence. He has attained full consciousness that his Self manifests as the universe and motivates the varied activities of his senses, mind, and intellect. The Self moves his outbreath and inbreath and pulses in his outer and inner perceptions. He realizes, "Everything is Śiva."

चितिः स्वतन्त्रा विश्वसिद्धिहेतुः

citiḥ svatantrā viśvasiddhihetuḥ

Citi creates the universe of Her own free will.

Pratyabhijñāhṛdayam 1

Citi is supremely free. She is self-revealing. She is the only cause of the creation, sustenance, and dissolution of the universe. She exists, holding within Her the power that creates, sustains, and destroys. The prime cause of everything, She is also the means to highest bliss. All forms, all places, and all instants of time are manifested from Her. She is all-pervading, always completely full, and composed of everlasting light. Manifesting as the universe, still She remains established in Her indivisibility and unity. Within the blue light, She pulsates as ambrosial bliss. There is nothing apart from Her. There is no one like Her. She is only One, the supreme witness, the One who is called cosmic Consciousness or supreme Śiva. She is ever solitary. In the beginning, in the middle, and in the end, only Citi is. She does not depend on any other agency; She is Her own basis and support. As She alone exists, She is in perfect freedom.

Desiring to create, She expands Herself of Her own free will. She manifests differences in Her being, appearing in countless forms and shapes. In a person this conscious spirit becomes the gross, subtle, causal, and supracausal bodies; the five sheaths;[6] the four states; and the fourfold psychic instrument. She becomes the five elements and combines them to make different life-forms.[7] She becomes the 72,000 subtle channels (*nāḍīs*), the seven bodily constituents,[8] the five vital airs and their functions, also the parts of the body from head to toe.

She expresses Herself as pleasure and pain, happiness and sorrow; as fear, disease, and agitation; as childhood and youth; as heaven and hell. Creating all things, She infuses them with Her spirit. Though Citi becomes the universe in this manner, still She does not discard Her transcendent aspect in which She remains always exactly the same—full of light, pure and untainted. In Her transcendent aspect, She is detached from the waking state and the good and bad actions performed in it. She is detached from all the events of the dream state. She is detached from the void of deep sleep. She dwells in the supracausal, transcendental state, transcending even that. She is pure awareness. Living in and as the universe, She is also apart from it as its eternal witness.

स्वेच्छया स्वभित्तौ विश्वम् उन्मीलयति

svecchayā svabhittau viśvam unmīlayati

By the power of Her own will alone, She unfolds the universe upon Her own screen.

Pratyabhijñāhṛdayam 2

The supreme Śiva, by His own free will, projects in Himself this universe where all beings live. Citi is the ground on which the universe is supported. Yet the universe and Citi are essentially one. There is no other material cause of creation. God, by His own free will, unceasingly unfolds within Himself this universe with its abundance of names and forms. God, who enjoys supreme freedom, whose powers are infinite, needs no help to create a universe. He Himself becomes the universe within Himself.

Even when it reflects large and diverse things in itself, a clear mirror remains clear and pure, without undergoing even the slightest change in its nature. Similarly, the Lord does not suffer the least diminution of His fullness, divinity, and perfection even as He creates this variegated cosmos by His boundless might.

Realistically considered, God makes the world from the substance of His own being. So the world is not world but the Master of the world. Tukārām Mahārāj says, "Whatever form He may assume, whatever costume He may wear, whatever shape He may take, it is God who has pervaded these infinite forms and costumes."

चितिरेव चेतनपदादवरूढाचेत्यसंकोचिनी चित्तम्

citireva cetanapadādavarūḍhācetyasaṃkocinī cittam

Citi Herself, descending from the plane of pure Consciousness, becomes the mind by contracting in accordance with the object perceived.

Pratyabhijñāhṛdayam 5

This aphorism is the very lifeblood of sadhana. It is priceless. If a seeker could understand this aphorism alone and believe in its truth, meditation would come to him by itself, and so would knowledge.

Citi descends from Her true condition, from pure Consciousness, assumes the forms of the objects She perceives, contracts Herself, and becomes the mind. It is essential to know the truth about the mind: the mind is full of Citi. If you don't understand this, you will not be able to steady the mind no matter how much you try.

Often an aspirant looks for answers in books and toils interminably to control his mind. He exhausts himself in his attempts at suppression, only to find that he is as far away from controlling the mind as he was when he started. Every day his mind grows in restlessness and turbulence. He falls into a despair so black that he renounces the spiritual path, convinced that the mind is impossible to subdue. In this despair, he dissipates all that he had gained through yoga.

A yogi should ponder the nature of this mind he is trying to stabilize. What exactly is it? Of what substance is it made? How does it come into existence? How can it be overcome? It is essential to grapple with these questions. Awareness of the mind's nature is the root of yoga, meditation, and all spiritual disciplines. Meditation will not be far from one who has acquired true knowledge of the mind, and equal vision will quickly follow.

In his commentary on this *sūtrā*, Śrī Kṣemarāja says:

न चित्तं नाम अन्यत्
किञ्चित् अपि तु सैव भगवती तत्

na cittaṃ nāma anyat kiñcit api tu saiva bhagavatī tat

The mind is nothing but
another name of Goddess Citi.

The mind is not a substance or an object or an attitude or the void. It is neither inert nor is it lethargic. It is Goddess Citi, Consciousness, the Śiva-Śakti who lives in Paraśiva and shares His nature fully. Citi is the glorious supreme Śakti. And this same Citi is the mind. She is Rāma's Sītā, Kṛṣṇa's Rādhā, the Gaurī of Paraśiva, the grace-bestowing power of God. She is the dynamic Kuṇḍalinī, the revered Goddess of yogis. She is the nature of the supreme being, the eternal throb of the Self. The great Goddess Citi is called the mind as She takes on the forms of outer objects to function in the outer world. To carry on worldly life, She descends from Her true nature, accepts limitation, and becomes worldly.

When Citi covers Herself with the three *guṇas,* She becomes the mind. When She transcends the *guṇas* and attains the knowledge of Her own essential nature, She is pure Citi, pure Consciousness.

The true lord of yoga is the yogi who is full of faith and devotion for his Guru and who possesses the eye of knowledge. He sees the thoughts and fantasies pulsing in his mind in their endless variety as the external throbs of the Self. He is anchored in the state of supreme divinity even in the midst of mental activity. The *Īśvarapratyabhijñā Kārikā* says:

विकल्पानं प्रस्रेऽपि महेशता

vikalpānaṃ prasre'pi maheśatā

[The yogi] retains his divinity even in the midst
of various thoughts and fantasies. [2.12]

Such an eye is obtained by the Guru's grace. The aspirant can then see directly that it is his own inner Self that becomes the mind as well as the multitude of sense objects.

मृत्कार्यभूतोऽपि मृदो न भिन्नः

mṛtkāryabhūto'pi mṛdo na bhinnaḥ

[Clay is not different from that
which is made of clay.]

A clay pot is still clay, and a gold ornament is still gold. In the same way, the outer expansion of the Self that appears as the world is still the Self. As soon as one realizes this, he passes into meditation spontaneously; this is the natural meditation one receives from the Guru. The mind itself is the universe. The mind itself is the Master of the universe.

चिद्वत् तच्छक्तिसंकोचात् मला वृतः संसारी

cidvat tacchaktisaṃkocāt malā vṛtaḥ saṃsārī

Universal Consciousness [Citi], because of contraction, becomes an ordinary being, subject to limitations.

Pratyabhijñāhṛdayam 9

The truth is that the highest Lord, pure Consciousness, lives in absolute freedom. He is all-pervading and all-knowing. By His glorious Śakti, He can do whatever He likes at any time. If an emperor wants to enact the role of an ordinary constable, he puts aside his pomp and majesty, his elephants and horses, and plays a commoner for a while. In exactly the same way, when the supreme Lord, who is pure Consciousness, sheds His undifferentiated state and accepts differences, then His unlimited powers of will, knowledge, and action appear to have shrunk. This is the state of ordinary people who are subject to limitations. By contraction of His power of action, the omnipotent One can only accomplish certain things. In this diminished state, he is dependent on his organs of action, and he becomes involved in performing good and evil deeds. This is *kārmamala,* the limitation of the power of action.

There are three such limitations. In brief, *āṇavamala* is the limitation by which an awareness of imperfection — so alien to the essential nature of Śiva — arises in His perfect being. *Māyīyamala* involves a sense of differentiation, of seeing things as different from one another and from Himself, that arises in the all-pervading Lord, the One-without-a-second. *Kārmamala* is an entanglement with good and bad actions, noble and evil undertakings.

When Śakti contracts, the highest Consciousness becomes bound by these three limitations. Then the Lord experiences His primal powers of omniscience, omnipotence, perfection, everlastingness, and all-pervasiveness in a reduced condition. This is poverty of Śakti; it is the experience of all creatures caught in the transmigratory cycle. The grace of the Guru rids the aspirant of his apparent Śakti-poverty, and his limited power begins to evolve. As soon as the great Kuṇḍalinī, Śiva's own Śakti, unfolds completely, Śiva once again experiences Himself as Śiva, and the bound individual becomes the supreme Lord. In the heart, the awareness "I am imperfect" dissolves into "I am perfect." This is the state of one who is liberated while living, one who revels unceasingly in the awareness "I am Śiva."

तथापि तद्वत् पञ्चकृत्यानि करोति

tathāpi tadvat pañcakṛtyāni karoti

Even in that state, he [the embodied soul]
performs the five processes.

Pratyabhijñāhṛdayam 10

The perfect Śiva, in His state of perfection, is always at play, carrying on the five processes for the upliftment of His devotees. Śrī Kṣemarāja praises the supreme Lord in this way:

नमः शिवाय सततं पञ्चकृत्यविधायिने ।
चिदानन्दघन स्वात्म परमार्थ विभासिने ॥

namaḥ śivāya satataṃ pañcakṛtyavidhāyine /
cidānandaghana svātma paramārtha vibhāsine //

Salutations to supreme Śiva who ceaselessly carries
on the sport of the five grand processes [creation, sustenance,
dissolution, concealment, and grace]. He continually
reveals the true nature of the highest reality.

Pratyabhijñāhṛdayam Invocation

God is Consciousness and bliss and ever one with His nature. Still, He assumes the five processes for sport. Similarly God, in bondage as the embodied soul, always carries out the five processes on a small scale.

The *Svacchanda Tantra* says that God's nature, even in the state of bondage, is Consciousness. The Lord takes on a body, *prāṇa,* and sense organs of His own will and acts accordingly. He manifests the same objects outside that flash in His awareness within Him. He performs the five processes in a limited way with limited power. When God, acting in the outer world through body, *prāṇa,* and senses, perceives different objects in different instants of time and at different points of space, that is creation. Sustenance is the perceiving of an object for a length of time. Dissolution is the disappearance of an object into the mind, as when one object is replaced in awareness by another. Concealment of its true nature comes about when undifferentiated Consciousness differentiates itself into manifold forms. To vibrate once again as pure undifferentiated light, after manifesting as diverse objects, is grace or revelation. This interesting subject is discussed in great detail in the *Spandasaṃdoha*.

There is an important difference between the doctrine of Brahman, held by the followers of Vedānta, and this philosophy of Self-recognition. According to Vedānta, Brahman is the cause of the universe; He is ever pure, awake, and free. He is bliss. But the world is false, the result of ignorance. Only Brahman is real, and one becomes Brahman when false knowledge is replaced by true. On the other hand, the philosophy of Self-recognition teaches that the world is not false. Emanating from supreme Śiva, it runs by His will. By His will also He withdraws it one day. Paraśiva is in need of no other materials to create the universe; He constantly carries out the five functions. In just the way that Śiva is the supreme creator and destroyer of the universe, the individual self continually performs the five processes in a limited way. Creation, sustenance, destruction, concealment, and grace are continually going on, both on the cosmic level and on the individual level. Meditate on them. Everyone is conscious of the various functions of the mind: if one were to dwell on the five processes just a little, they would reveal their significance.

We perceive an object at a certain instant of time, a certain point in space, and in a certain form. At the same time, we grasp its color and other characteristics. In the moment of perception we create the object; its appearance in our mind is its creation therein. When the image of a cow vibrates in the mind, the cow is created; the thought of a bridge is the creation of that bridge. Thus, whatever throbs in our mind comes into existence. When an object in the mind is replaced by another, the space, time, substance, and form all change. The cow that had been created is gone, replaced by, say, an elephant; that is the cow's destruction in the mind.

An object exists as long as we perceive it without any break; it may be for a moment or longer. If the image of the elephant remains in our mind for twenty minutes, we have sustained it for that amount of time.

When the objects that are undifferentiated within Citi appear as different entities, that is concealment of Citi's true nature. When, after hearing and seeing many different objects, we suddenly become aware of their identity with Consciousness, we accomplish the fifth task: grace. Grace is nothing but seeing objects as one with self-luminous Citi, even though they may appear to be different.

Yogis remain aware, with unwavering faith, of the continual flow of thoughts and the five processes within their minds. The seeker who becomes aware of his own authorship of the five acts achieves the divine state. It is said, for this reason, that those who, on receiving grace, continually contemplate Consciousness or Paraśiva within themselves become *jīvanmuktas.* They regard this cosmos as an expansion of their own Self. Though such a person may appear to be bound because he possesses body, *prāṇa,* and senses, he is in truth a free soul. But those who consider the objects of perception to be different from the Self forever remain in bondage.

सृष्टिसंहारकर्तारं विलयस्थितिकारकं ।
अनुग्रहकरं देवं प्रणतार्ति विनाशनम् ॥

sṛṣṭisaṃhārakartāraṃ vilayasthitikārakaṃ /
anugrahakaraṃ devaṃ praṇatārti vināśanam //

The Lord is the author of creation, sustenance,
destruction, concealment, and grace. He removes
the suffering of those who take refuge in Him.

Svacchanda Tantra 1.3

Paraśiva is full of affection for His devotees. He destroys their sorrow, poverty, ignorance, and darkness, and He helps them through crises. For their protection He continually holds His sport, enacting the drama of the five processes. The five processes exhibit His splendor, and He works through them to promote the welfare of his devotees in every part of the universe. The wise man contemplates the processes within himself and is soon intoxicated, identifying himself with Śiva. He sits calmly and watches the various thoughts arise in his mind. Citi Herself becomes these thoughts. In the boundless expanse of Her blissful Consciousness, She creates and dissolves countless worlds. This is Her wonderful play.

तत् परिज्ञाने चित्तम् एव अन्तर्मुखीभावेन
चेतनपदाध्यारोहात् चितिः

tat parijñāne cittam eva antarmukhībhāvena
cetanapadādhyārohāt citiḥ

Attaining full knowledge of that [the fivefold act],
the mind turns within, rises to the plane
of pure Consciousness, and becomes Citi.

Pratyabhijñāhṛdayam 13

Citi becomes the mind when She turns Her eyes from Her own nature and becomes involved in the external world and its affairs. The mind, having acquired full knowledge of the five processes of creation, sustenance, dissolution, concealment, and grace—which go on within by themselves—follows the path of meditation initiated by the Guru and turns within. Interest in meditation increases, and the awareness of external objects dissolves proportionately. The mind, penetrating its own depths, obtains inner knowledge, this inward-directed movement merging the mind into the Self. Resting in the Self, the mind rises again to the plane of Consciousness, Citi. This is the culmination of sadhana, when the mind melts into total awareness, perfect bliss, and full contentment.

स्वशक्तिविकासे तु शिव एव

svaśaktivikāse tu śiva eva

On the unfolding of Śakti, one becomes Śiva.

Having become alienated from its source and taken on the form of objects, the light of Consciousness turns within and one's Śakti is unfolded. The aspirant rests in the Self, the state of Śiva. This is the rightful homeland. The people who can see beyond call it the religion of man and the great spiritual pilgrimage.

The mind filled with objects and roaming in the outer world possessed by differences is in the reduced condition of the embodied soul, in the bondage of ignorance. When by Guru's grace this same mind looks within in meditation, the journey is redirected from ignorance to knowledge, from bondage to liberation, from birth and death to *jīvanmukti,* from sin and sorrow to the most sacred absorption in Brahman. All differences are merged into the sole undifferentiated identity, and thus one becomes Paraśiva. One should meditate all the time.

बललाभे विश्वम् आत्मसात्करोति

balalābhe viśvam ātmasātkaroti

By acquiring the power of Citi,
the aspirant assimilates the universe into himself.

Pratyabhijñāhṛdayam 15

In this context, *power* means the awareness "I am the Soul of the universe." With the attainment of this awareness, the universe, which had appeared so alien, becomes one's own. By the power of the Guru, the holiest deity, the great Kuṇḍalinī Śakti, is fully awakened in the seeker, and Siddha Yoga is activated within him. He overcomes limitation and becomes conscious of the unity of his Self with the universe as his innermost nature reveals itself. This is true power. By the power of the Guru's grace, he ceases to regard the universe, from Sadāśiva to the earth, as separate from himself.[9] All objects, animate and inanimate, are now only different forms of Citi. He merges his individual identity into Citi, becoming one with the cosmos.

We can see that in normal life a person who thinks of himself as small or lonely or weak, lacking in skill or strength, a victim of sorrow and misery, actually lives in a wretched state. By the grace of the Guru, such a person can throw off his sense of weakness and inferiority. As Siddha Yoga works in him by the Guru's power, he rises to the awareness of his identity with the universe and makes it his own.

मध्यविकासाच् चिदानन्दलाभः

madhyavikāsāc cidānandalābhaḥ

By the unfoldment of the center (*madhya*),
the bliss of Consciousness is acquired.

Pratyabhijñāhṛdayam 17

The infinitely powerful and glorious Goddess Saṃvitti (supreme Consciousness) is the true center of this animate and inanimate universe. She dwells within all things, pervading them in subtle form. Without Her grace, no one can realize his real nature. She involves Herself, of Her own free will, in the sportful maze of Her own making and manifests all the shapes and forms that fill the universe. Assuming *prāṇa,* intellect, and all the other organs and emanating thousands of *nāḍīs,* She fashions the human body. The great Śakti pervades the body, particularly its central *nāḍī, suṣumṇā,* which extends from the *sahasrāra,* situated in the middle of the *brahmarandhra* at the top of the head, to the *mūlādhāra* at the base of the spine. She supports both Brahman and *prāṇaśakti* therein. All our thoughts, feelings, and inspirations spring from the central *nāḍī* and subside in it. The mind arises from Brahman and vibrates into thoughts by the power of *prāṇa,* the life force. One who lacks Guru's grace is ignorant of these secrets.

Goddess Saṃvitti, Citi Śakti, expresses Herself in countless ways, assuming countless shapes and forms. She fills the whole gross and subtle cosmos. She is the indweller in all creatures, beyond the grasp of the senses. She makes the body—consisting of seven constituents and 72,000 *nāḍīs*—and enters it as *prāṇa.* She is present everywhere in the body in subtle form. There She causes *prāṇa* to move through the *nāḍīs* at lightning speed. She circulates blood in a systematic manner.

Of the 72,000 *nāḍīs,* one hundred are important. Of these hundred, ten are very important. Of these ten, three are outstanding. And of these three, one is the most significant. That is the *suṣumṇā nāḍī*, the *brahma nāḍī*, the *saṃvitti nāḍī*, the *madhya nāḍī*, or the pathway of the great Kuṇḍalinī. All the other *nāḍīs* are supported by it. The various good and evil thoughts and feelings such as love, devotion, attachment, and hatred appear from and disappear into it.

Though the central *nāḍī* extends from the *sahasrāra* to the *mūlādhāra*, one remains unaware of it without Guru's grace. Only by receiving shaktipat through Guru's grace is the central *nāḍī* unfolded. This is followed by purification of the *nāḍīs*, of the seven bodily constituents, and of the mind. In the end, the aspirant becomes centered in the *sahasrāra*. In other words, from being human he becomes God; from *jīva* (an individual creature) he becomes Śiva. Then he sees directly that all mental states, all salutary and harmful mental movements—the consciousness of one's divinity and the consciousness of a limited existence, as well as identification with the Guru and with Śiva—all these arise and dissolve by the power of Saṃvitti spreading through the central *nāḍī*. Only he is a true meditator, a truly enlightened being, who has attained this knowledge.

If the central *nāḍī* is not unfolded, a person cannot evolve. The unfolding of the central *nāḍī* is an aspirant's pilgrimage, his path of Self-realization.

मनुषम् देहमास्थयच्छनऽस्ते परमेश्वरः

manuṣaṃ dehamāsthayacchana'ste parameśvaraḥ

The supreme Lord secretly enters the human body and dwells in it.

What the Śaivite sage Utpaladeva says here is true, and what a wonder it is! Man commits a major blunder when he does not try to find out who it is that lives in his body. The Lord says in the *Bhagavadgītā*:

क्षेत्रज्ञं चापि मां विद्धि सर्वक्षेत्रेषु भारत

kṣetrajñaṃ cāpi māṃ viddhi sarvakṣetreṣu bhārata

Know Me to be the Knower of the field in all fields. [13.2]

In other words, the Lord is telling Arjuna, I am that Knower who dwells in all the fields as Knower of the field. The body is called a field since the fruits of all actions are reaped there; all consequences, good and bad, are experienced there. God, the Self, dwells in the body as a witness, watching what occurs there without being moved.

यथा च भगवान् विश्वशरीरः

yathā ca bhagavān viśvaśarīraḥ

The universe is God's body.

Long ago Lord Śiva replied to a question by the sage Maitreya in this way:

देहो देवालयः प्रोक्तो आत्मा केवलः शिवः

deho devālayaḥ prokto ātmā kevalaḥ śivaḥ

This body is the holiest temple
because supreme Śiva abides in it as its Self.

When wise Naciketas asked where he could find God, Yama said:

अशरीरं शरीरेषु अनवस्थेषु अवस्थितम् ।
महान्तं विभुम् आत्मानं मत्वा धीरो न शोचति ॥

aśarīraṃ śarīreṣu anavastheṣu avasthitam /
mahāntaṃ vibhum ātmānaṃ matvā dhīro na śocati //

God lives in all bodies and is yet without a body.
He is the eternal and unmoving reality behind all fleeting
and moving things. He is supreme. He is all-pervading. By seeing
Him in meditation, one becomes steady, courageous, discerning,
and free from sorrow, and attains the highest peace.

Kaṭha Upaniṣad 1.2.22

There is no deity like the Self, no temple like the body, no *japa* like *So'ham*, no worship like meditation. There is no mother or father like Śrī Nityananda, no spiritual doctrine like Self-recognition.

आत्मादधिकं किम् अस्ति तत्त्वम्

ātmādadhikaṃ kim asti tattvam

Is there anything greater than the Self?

Even a momentary awareness that God functions through one's body is attended by great peace. The supreme Lord is indeed the dweller in the body. The *Īśvarapratyabhijñā* says:

सर्वो ममायं विभव इत्येवं परिजनातः ।
विश्वात्मनो विकल्पानां प्रसरेऽपि महेशता ॥

sarvo mamāyaṃ vibhava ityevaṃ parijanātaḥ /
viśvātmano vikalpānāṃ prasare'pi maheśatā //

The yogi who knows that the entire splendor
of the universe is his, who rises to the awareness of unity
with the universe, retains his divinity even in the midst
of various thoughts and fancies. [2.12]

Knowledge has great value. With right knowledge, meditation is not so difficult. Without it, the mind is afflicted by suffering and will not become still to meditate. Therefore, *jīvanmukti* is not far from the one who has attained the knowledge of the true nature of the universe, its various component objects and their modifications, and of the mind and its countless images and ideas.

What is the universe? Supreme Śiva has Himself become earth, water, fire, air, space, rivers, oceans, and various bodies. The same nameless One pervades countless names and forms. The beauty of the infinite cosmos is the Self's own glory, its own beauty. Whatever the figures painted on a canvas, whatever the style, they are the creation of the same painter, using the same brush, the same colors, the same power of conception. Just so, the maker of the whole cosmos is Śiva; it is made in Śiva—the paints, brushes, and canvas are all Śiva. From the Guru's viewpoint, all that exists is Paraśiva manifesting only Himself. Baba Nityananda used to say, "Your father is Brahman, your mother is Brahman, you are Brahman. All are Brahman. Everything is Brahman. Where else do you look for Him?"

He who knows that this visible creation is the splendor of his own Self is not disturbed from his natural, liberated state, even when thoughts and fancies move in his mind. To him all these and the substance of which they are made are nothing but vibrations of Paraśiva. Considering all space, time, and forms to be the sport of universal Consciousness, he attains the state of divinity even in the midst of mental activity. All his thoughts are Śiva, his fancies are Śiva, his agitation and even its consequences are also Śiva. Regarding everything as the glory of his own Self, he remains tranquil. The awareness of the splendor of the Self is the state of Maheśvara, the great Lord. This awareness is indeed meditation. To see every pulsation of the mind as a ray of Citi is meditation of a high order.

तस्माच् छब्दार्थचिन्तासु न सावस्था न या शिवः

tasmāc chabdārthacintāsu na sāvasthā na yā śivaḥ

There are no sounds, meanings, or thoughts that are not Śiva.

Spanda Kārikā 2.4

The Lord originally manifested Himself as sound—*ādau bhagavān śabdarāśiḥ.* All the letters of the Sanskrit alphabet, from *a* to *kṣa,* being supreme Śiva, originated from *Oṃ. Oṃ* is Paraśiva, the supreme Lord. The saints and sages have attained full God-realization through the worship of Brahman as the Name.

शब्द ब्रह्मेति यच्छेदं शास्त्रम्

śabda brahmeti yacchedaṃ śāstram

The scriptures say that sound is Brahman.

All birds and animals communicate through their own sound-language, making sounds that are understood by other creatures. People commune with their fellow beings through speech. Speech consists of sentences; sentences are formed by words; words are a combination of letters; letters are nothing but sounds. Before they are uttered, sounds exist in the unmanifest state. They are both different and not different from Śakti. Subtly considered, they are one with Śakti, which is also known as Paraśakti.

All sounds are Śiva. All meanings conveyed by sounds are Śiva. All thoughts arising from sounds are Śiva. There is not a single sound that is not Śiva, not a single meaning different from Śiva, who is all knowledge. There is not a single thought that is apart from the mind, and the mind is Citi or Śiva. Sounds, meanings, and thoughts are all Śiva. Even that which appears to be distinct from Śiva is nothing but Śiva.

इति वा यस्य संवित्तिः क्रीडात्वेनाखिलं जगत् ।
स पश्यन् सततं युक्तो जीवन्मुक्तो न संशयः ।।

iti vā yasya saṃvittiḥ krīḍātvenākhilaṃ jagat /
sa paśyan satataṃ yukto jīvanmukto na saṃśayaḥ //

This entire universe is a sport of universal Consciousness.
One who is constantly aware of this truth is
undoubtedly liberated in this very life.

Spanda Kārikā 2.5

In fact, this universe is not a universe. It is not an illusion as the illusionists hold. It is neither the void nor atoms nor nature nor a modification of some basic substance. Though it appears to be matter—appears to be earth, water, fire, air, and ether—it is only the play of Citi and the sport of Kuṇḍalinī. It is the blissful self-unfolding of Consciousness. It is the play of the many from the One and the One in the many. Behind the differences lies the undifferentiated; the undifferentiated manifests differences. It is the nondual becoming dual and reveling in that play. Differences lie not in the objective universe but in the veil that covers the eye that sees. The lotion of the Guru's grace rends that veil and gives the yogi the eye to see truth. The yogi is bound only as long as he apprehends the play of Consciousness as the universe. When there is no universe, how can there be bondage? The moment the concept of *universe* is eliminated, one becomes a *jīvanmukta,* a being who is liberated in this life.

नाशिवं विद्यते क्वचित्

nāśivaṃ vidyate kvacit

Nothing that is not Śiva exists anywhere.

Svacchanda Tantra

Śiva pervades everything without being different from anything. How can anything be other than Śiva? Paraśakti Citi spreads everywhere in the universe; She is matter in material objects and consciousness in conscious beings. She takes on attributes, yet She is without attributes. It is She who is sporting everywhere. How can there be anything different from Her? In the universe that is only Citi's play, what can be impure or unclean?

They alone are without Śiva who see this universe, which is Śiva, as being without Śiva.

A person's ignorance makes him impure, a sinner, a vile creature. He projects his own loathsomeness on others, arrogating their purity to himself. Seeing his own projection of hell, he exclaims, "That one is without Śiva." To think that anything can ever exist that is without Śiva is the vision of a blind man—dark confusion.

That which the ignorant see as the phenomenal universe is in reality the playful outer manifestation of Consciousness. What can be done if a deluded person thinks that a rope is a snake? The snake and the fear, the trembling, the stuttering speech, the palpitation of the heart caused by its appearance are illusion. The rope alone is the immutable truth. The imagined snake is the sport of the rope.

Śiva is the is-ness of everything. Śiva is real. Śiva is all-pervading. He never ceases to exist. He never vanishes. He is eternal whether or not He is perceived to be so. He is everything. He is in the fallen in the same measure as in the redeemed. He is as much in the wicked as in the enlightened; as much in the sinner as in the saint; as much in an atom as in the vast cosmos; as much in a drop as in an ocean. He is beyond all limitations of space, time, and substance. He is everywhere. He is everlasting. He is in all. He is ever perfect. Indeed, to think that nothing is without Śiva is to see Śiva.

PART TWO

Vijñānabhairava

A NOTE ON THE *VIJÑĀNABHAIRAVA*

These are Swami Muktananda's contemplations on eighteen verses from the *Vijñānabhairava* ("The Knowledge of the Lord"). This is an Āgamic text from about the seventh century that is cited in numerous places by the authors of other Kashmiri Śaiva texts, indicating that its *dhāraṇās*, concentration exercises, have long been spiritual practices among the Śaivites of Kashmir. Here Baba extols the explicit power of mantra to bring about *vijñāna* (experiential knowledge) of Bhairava, the Lord of the inner Self of all. In particular, Baba presents the practice of the internal mantra *Haṃsa,* "I am That."

Written in 1979, these poetic discussions—in some cases, renderings—of the *Vijñānabhairava* are being published for the first time.

—*Swami Shantananda*

शक्तिशक्तिमतोर् यद्वद् अभेदः सर्वदा स्थितः ।
अतस् तद्धर्मधर्मित्वात् पराशक्तिः परात्मनः ।।
न वह्नेर् दाहिका शक्तिः व्यतिरिक्ता विभाव्याव्यते ।
केवलं ज्ञानसत्तायां प्रारम्भोऽयम् प्रवेशने ।।

śaktiśaktimator yadvad abhedaḥ sarvadā sthitaḥ /
atas taddharmadharmitvāt parāśaktiḥ parātmanaḥ //
na vahner dāhikā śaktiḥ vyatiriktā vibhāvyate /
kevalaṃ jñānasattāyāṃ prārambho'yam praveśane //

Vijñānabhairava 18-19

The One who belongs to all—in water, the Self of the water; in earth, the Self of the earth; in fire, the Self of the fire; in air, the Self of the air; in ether, the Self of the ether—is the conscious Self in the heart. I offer the love of my soul to the Self of the universe, the embodiment of auspiciousness.

The One who reveals His own Śakti in the form of words to facilitate mundane activities also manifests as objects—I offer infinite love to that conscious Self.

Consciousness, becoming the Self of words, reveals the world. It becomes unity, diversity, and unity in diversity. The supreme principle is both the word and its meaning. The *Vijñānabhairava* recognizes it in the form of Śiva and Śakti.

The One who has become the word and its meaning in order to unfold the activities of the entire world, who makes possible the works of all philosophers, is the Lord of Pārvatī. He is our own Self. And He is the *Vijñānabhairava.*

Without knowing Him, perfect knowledge cannot be attained. Knowing Him, everything else is known. He is the pure and independent Self. So says the *Vijñānabhairava.*

Śiva and Śakti are not two, but the One described in two ways. Man and his conscious Śakti are referred to as Bhairava. Śakti or Citi Śakti is the power that creates the universe.

As the heat of fire and its power to burn are not different from fire, so Śakti, the soul of Bhairava, is not different from Consciousness, the supreme principle. So says the *Vijñānabhairava.*

शक्त्यवस्थाप्रविष्टस्य निर्विभागेन भावना ।
तदासौ शिवरूपी स्याच् शैवी मुखम् इहोच्यते ॥
यथालोकेन दीपस्य किरणैर् भास्करस्य च ।
ज्ञायते दिग्विभागादि तद्वच् छक्त्या शिवः प्रिये ॥

śaktyavasthāpraviṣṭasya nirvibhāgena bhāvanā /
tadāsau śivarūpī syāt śaivī mukham ihocyate //
yathālokenadīpasya kiraṇair bhāskarasya ca /
jñāyate digvibhāgādi tadvac chaktyā śivaḥ priye //

Vijñānabhairava 20-21

By means of its own power, Consciousness is known. Śiva and Śakti are one and inseparable. Only by means of Paraśakti can Śiva, Consciousness, and unity be attained. So says the *Vijñānabhairava.*

The supreme Self is absolutely independent and unknowable, yet it is the self-effulgent Knower of all. The term *bhairava* refers to knowledge of That.

As a flame illumines both itself and all around it, so the sun illumines both itself and this entire world. It is self-effulgent. The One who illumines Himself is the *Vijñānabhairava.*

The sun is illumined by the brilliance of its own rays. Just as to see a flame a second flame is not needed, or to see the sun a second sun is not needed, so the One who illumines and comprehends Himself with His own knowledge is the Self, Consciousness. So says the *Vijñānabhairava.*

श्री देवी उवाच
देवदेव त्रिशूलाङ्क कपालकृतभूषण ।
दिग्देशकालशून्या च व्यपदेशविवर्जिता ।।
यावस्था भरिताकारा भैरवस्योपलभ्यते ।
कैर् उपायैर् मुखं तस्य परादेवी कथं भवेत् ।।
यथा सम्यग् अहं वेद्मि तथा मे ब्रूहि भैरव ।

śrī devī uvāca
devadeva triśūlāṅka kapālakṛtabhūṣaṇa /
digdeśakālaśūnyā ca vyapadeśavivarjitā //
yāvasthā bharitākārā bhairavasyopalabhyate /
kair upāyair mukhaṃ tasya parādevī kathaṃ bhavet //
yathā samyag ahaṃ vedmi tathā me brūhi bhairava /

Vijñānabhairava 22-23

Bhairavī entreats Bhairava:

Reveal the knowledge of the simplest means to find You, as You exist naturally in me and in all.

Reveal a complete sadhana comprising the essence of all self-effort. It should be full of perfect happiness; it should be attainable with a minimum of strain; it should bear great fruit. With the knowledge of That, perfect bliss should arise. After attaining That, all fear should vanish. After realizing That, no difficult birth should follow. Who is that *Vijñānabhairava*?

Where there is no fear of death, where pain and sorrow cannot enter, where the journey of yogis is consummated, where the wisdom of *jñānīs* becomes firm, where all religions end—O *Vijñānabhairava*, reveal the wisdom of that sadhana!

श्रीभैरव उवाच
उर्ध्वे प्राणो ह्यधो जीवो विसर्गात्मा परोच्चरेत् ।
उत्पत्तिद्वितयस्थाने भरणाद् भरिता स्थितिः ।।

śrībhairava uvāca
ūrdhve prāṇo hyadho jīvo visargātmā paroccaret /
utpattidvitayasthāne bharaṇād bharitā sthitiḥ //

Vijñānabhairava 24

Lord Bhairava replies:

The exhalation that goes forth from the heart to a distance of twelve fingers and the inhalation, or *jīva*, that returns from that distance to the heart are the voice of the pulsation of Parādevī. She Herself, vibrating in the form of outbreath and inbreath, constantly utters the sounds of the breath.

This Parādevī, Citi Kuṇḍalinī, which is vibration, manifests the outer creation within us. This is Her inherent nature. A yogi knows Bhairava by experiencing the first vibration of His Śakti as it continually arises in both the heart and the *dvādaśānta*, the sources of the outgoing and incoming breaths.

The breath enters with the sound *ham* and goes forth with the sound *so*. Day and night it repeats these sounds. The place where *ham* merges is the *madhyadaśā*. When *ham* has merged totally and *so* has not yet arisen, that instant is the *madhyadaśā*. The Lord of the Self is there. Know Him, O Devī! He is the *Vijñānabhairava*.

मरुतोऽन्तर् बहिर् वापि वियद्युग्मानिवर्तनात् ।
भैरव्या भैरवस्येत्थं भैरवि व्यज्यते वपुः ॥

marutoʼntar bahir vāpi viyadyugmānivartanāt /
bhairavyā bhairavasyettham bhairavi vyajyate vapuḥ //

Vijñānabhairava 25

Inside, in the heart, the *jīva,* or inhalation, merges and arises with the sound *ham*; outside, at a distance of twelve fingers, the exhalation arises and merges with the sound *so.* In the stillness of both these *madhyadaśās,* find the realm of the Self. To let your mind merge there is sadhana, the *Vijñānabhairava.*

In the *Bhagavadgītā* the Lord says, "I dwell in the hearts of all beings. I make everyone dance." I am the inner *ham,* which is Śiva, the supreme principle. The outer *so* is Śakti, who makes the mind frolic. Śiva is Śakti; Śakti is Śiva. The *Vijñānabhairava* says both are one.

Ham is *so*; *so* is *ham.* Śiva is Śakti; Śakti is Śiva. The mystery of both is knowledge, devotion, and liberation. With a pure intellect, always know the spontaneous *japa* in the heart. That is perfection. That is enlightenment. That is the bliss of Consciousness, the *Vijñānabhairava.*

Listen, O Bhairavī. When the wandering mind ceases for an instant at the inner space of the heart, the root of the outbreath and inbreath, or at the outer space at a distance of twelve fingers—that is the *madhyadaśā,* the place free from all thought.

The breath arises from the stalk of the heart lotus. By way of the nostrils it goes forth to a distance of twelve fingers. Finally it merges in this outer space, called the *dvādaśānta* by the knower of yoga. Inside and out, only the One exists, the *Vijñānabhairava.*

न व्रजेन् न विशेच् छक्तिर् मरुद्रूपा विकासिते ।
निर्विकल्पकतया मध्ये तया भैरवरूपता ॥

na vrajen na viśec chaktir marudrūpā vikāsite /
nirvikalpakatayā madhye tayā bhairavarūpatā //

Vijñānabhairava 26

The breath enters, stops, returns, stops outside, then enters again. This cessation is the natural *kumbhaka,* retention of breath. Spontaneous *kumbhaka* is effortless *prāṇāyāma.* The *jñānī,* the Guru, the knower of the truth, all call this the natural science of yoga.

Just as various reflections appear and disappear in a mirror, so both outer objects and inner stirrings of feeling arise and subside in the space of Consciousness. Entering the natural state of yoga, a yogi embraces all things and merges them in *samādhi.*

He who practices *samādhi* is constantly absorbed in the state in which the eyes look outward but the gaze is directed within. His eyes neither open nor close. He tastes the nectar of the experience of his own true nature in the *bhairavī mudrā,* which is concealed in all the Tantras. This is the yogi's state of supreme bliss.

कुम्भिता रेचिता वापि पूरिता वा यदा भवेत् ।
तदन्ते शान्तनामासौ शक्त्या शान्तः प्रकाशते ॥

kumbhitā recitā vāpi pūritā vā yadā bhavet /
tadante śāntanāmāsau śaktyā śāntaḥ prakāśate //

Vijñānabhairava 27

Once again, with the constant practice of external or internal *kumbhaka,* based on Śakti in the form of the outbreath and the inbreath, both become still and the *madhyadaśā* arises. When the state of illumination occurs, the image of the Self is revealed.

आमूलात् किरणाभासां सूक्ष्मात् सूक्ष्मतरात्मिकाम् ।
चिन्तयेत् तां द्विषट्कान्ते श्याम्यन्तीं भैरवोदयः ॥

āmūlāt kiraṇābhāsāṃ sūkṣmāt sūkṣmatarātmikām /
cintayet tāṃ dviṣaṭkānte śyāmyantīṃ bhairavodayaḥ //

Vijñānabhairava 28

Contemplate the awareness that extends from the heart to a distance of twelve fingers, shining like the sun and the moon, gradually growing more and more subtle. As this awareness reaches the *dvādaśānta,* it becomes still and free from name and attribute. It is the *madhyadaśā.* When he arrives there, a yogi attains the state of Bhairava.

उद्गच्छन्तीं तडित्रूपां प्रतिचक्रं क्रमात् क्रमम् ।
ऊर्ध्वं मुष्टित्रयं यावत् तावद् अन्ते महोदयः

udgacchantīṃ taḍitrūpāṃ praticakraṃ kramāt kramam /
ūrdhvaṃ muṣṭitrayaṃ yāvat tāvad ante mahodayaḥ //

Vijñānabhairava 29

After the arising of the *madhyadaśā,* contemplate the Śakti flashing like lightning in every successive *cakra,* from the base of the spine to the crown of the head. The Bhairava, the illuminator who lights the entire universe with His radiance, who lives in the *dvādaśānta,* shines.

क्रमद्वादशकं सम्यग् द्वादशाक्षरभेदितम् ।
स्थूलसूक्ष्मपरस्थित्या मुक्त्वा मुक्त्वान्ततः शिवः ॥

kramadvādaśakaṃ samyag dvādaśākṣarabheditam /
sthūlasūkṣmaparasthityā muktvā muktvāntataḥ śivaḥ //

Vijñānabhairava 30

When the mind is rapt in the *mūlādhāra* (the *kanda*), the navel, the heart, the throat, the palate, the space between the eyebrows, the forehead, or anywhere else inside up to the *brahmarandhra;*[10] when it is steadied in ether, in water, in forests, or somewhere else in the outer creation—then the supreme light blazes in the heart.

तयापूर्याशु मूर्धान्तं भङ्क्त्वा भ्रूक्षेपसेतुना ।
निर्विकल्पं मनः कृत्वा सर्वोर्ध्वे सर्वगोद्गमः ॥

tayāpūryāśu mūrdhāntaṃ bhaṅktvā bhrūkṣepasetunā /
nirvikalpaṃ manaḥ kṛtvā sarvordhve sarvagodgamaḥ //

Vijñānabhairava 31

The Self of the *jīva* is all, is the soul of all, is everywhere the form of the universe because it knows all objects and calls them into existence. The Self of the *jīva* is everything, for being the knower of all things, it is forever one with them in the form of knowledge. It can never be different from them.

प्रणवादिसमुच्चारात् प्लुतान्ते शून्यभावनात् ।
शून्यया परया शक्त्या शून्यताम् एति भैरवि ॥

praṇavādisamuccārāt plutānte śūnyabhāvanāt /
śūnyayā parayā śaktyā śūnyatām eti bhairavi //

Vijñānabhairava 39

By doing *japa* of the great primordial mantra, the *praṇava,* with devotion and understanding, the mind spontaneously enters the *madhyadaśā.* The Tantra *śāstra* enumerates three types of primordial sound: in the Vedic scriptures, *Oṃ;* in the Śaivite scriptures, *hūṃ;* and in the Śākta scriptures, *hrīṃ.*[11] By doing *japa* of these sounds, all difficulties are destroyed and deep meditation ensues.

यस्य कस्यापि वर्णस्य पूर्वान्तावनुभावयेत् ।
शून्यया शून्यभूतोऽसौ शून्याकारः पुमान् मवत् ॥

yasya kasyāpi varṇasya pūrvāntāvanubhāvayet /
śūnyayā śūnyabhūto'sau śūnyākāraḥ pumān bhavet //

Vijñānabhairava 40

The principle of the Self is also easily recognized by doing *japa* of the garland of letters of any other mantra. The goal of all mantras—*Rāma, Kṛṣṇa, Śiva*—is the Self. So says the *Vijñānabhairava.*

तन्त्र्यादिवाद्यशब्देषु दीर्घेषु क्रमसंस्थितेः ।
अनन्यचेताः प्रत्यन्ते परव्योमवपुर् भवेत् ॥

tantryādivādyaśabdeṣu dīrgheṣu kramasaṃsthiteḥ /
ananyacetāḥ pratyante paravyomavapur bhavet //

Vijñānabhairava 41

The *sādhaka* who concentrates his mind on the sounds of stringed instruments such as the *vīṇā,* tamboura, *saraṅgī,* and others becomes free from all diseases. By entering the inner realm, he becomes one with the Bhairava of knowledge, who is the space of Consciousness.

निजदेहे सर्वदिक्कं युगपद् भावयेद् वियत् ।
निर्विकल्पमनास् तस्य वियत् सर्वं प्रवर्तते ।।

nijadehe sarvadikkaṃ yugapad bhāvayed viyat /
nirvikalpamanās tasya viyat sarvaṃ pravartate //

Vijñānabhairava 43

The *sādhaka* who experiences the void beyond thought—above, below, to the right, to the left, and all around—realizes the state of Śiva, the abode of Consciousness. This Consciousness is everywhere.

PART THREE

Gurugītā

A NOTE ON THE *GURUGĪTĀ*

Swami Muktananda said of the *Gurugītā* that "it is the one indispensable text," and its verses are chanted in Siddha Yoga ashrams every morning as the sun rises. It is recommended as a subject for study and contemplation as well, since it is one of those rare scriptures in the mystical tradition of India exclusively dedicated to expounding the true nature of the Guru. This Sanskrit text is in the form of a dialogue between Lord Śiva and His consort, Pārvatī, giving it the characteristic flavor of an Āgama. In content, however, there is a confluence of the philosophical currents of both Śaivism and Vedānta. In the final colophon, the *Gurugītā* describes itself as a part of the *Skanda Purāṇa,* one of the collections of sacred lore in the scriptural tradition of India.

In these commentaries, Baba now moves from *jñānī* to *bhakta,* from scholar to ecstatic lover of God. Here he adopts the devotional style of the poet-saints whose songs he loved to sing, ending most of the commentaries with a couplet that speaks of his reverence for the supreme deity of the spiritual seeker, the *sadguru.*

—*Swami Shantananda*

आसनं शयनं वस्त्रं भूषणं वाहनादिकम् ॥
साधकेन प्रदातव्यं गुरुसन्तोषकारकम् ।

āsanaṃ śayanaṃ vastraṃ bhūṣaṇaṃ vāhanādikam //
sādhakena pradātavyaṃ gurusantoṣakārakam /

The aspirant should offer to the Guru a seat, a bed, clothes, ornaments, a vehicle, and other things that will please the Guru.

Gurugītā 26-27

Giving is a noble act, and the one who makes an offering secures whatever he desires. One becomes the master of that which he offers to the Guru. By giving a fine *āsana,* a meditation mat, he masters *āsana,* meditation posture. Giving a bed he will have many beds. By giving clothes he will have clothes in abundance, and when he gives jewelry he receives a treasure in return. It is essential that the Guru be pleased with the seeker, and so he should make an auspicious offering.

Offer everything to the Guru—
āsana, bed, clothes, ornaments,
along with your own self.
In return, drink him in
as eternal knowledge and experience.

गुरोर् आराधनं कार्यं स्वजीवित्वं निवेदयेत् ॥
कर्मणा मनसा वाचा नित्यम् आराधयेद् गुरुम् ।

gurorārādhanaṃ kāryaṃ svajīvitvaṃ nivedayet //
karmaṇā manasā vācā nityam ārādhayed gurum /

Dedicate your life to the Guru.
Worship the Guru at every moment,
in words, actions, and mind.

Gurugītā 27-28

The more a disciple pleases the Guru, the more the disciple's own joy increases. One who offers his very life to the Guru becomes the Guru. With the body, perform *guruseva*; mentally, contemplate the teachings of the Guru; and use the tongue to sing the Guru's praises.

The Guru's pleasure is your joy.
Offer up your life, give it to the Guru:
seva in your actions, contemplation by mind.
Sing the glory of his name with your speech,
O Muktananda.

शरीरम् इन्द्रियं प्राणान् सद्गुरुभ्यो निवेदयेत् ।
आत्मदारादिकं सर्वं सद्गुरुभ्यो निवेदयेत् ॥

śarīram indriyaṃ prāṇan sadgurubhyo nivedayet /
ātmadārādikaṃ sarvaṃ sadgurubhyo nivedayet //

Make a sacred offering of your body, senses, and *prāṇa* to the *sadguru*. Consecrate everything to the *sadguru*—your soul, your wife, everything.

Gurugītā 29

An aspirant who holds something back from the Guru will come to regret that. Once the body, the senses, the *prāṇa* have been offered to the spiritual Master, how can one's attachments to the world of change survive?

See the Guru in everything:
    your body, mind, and wealth.
Muktananda, know him as your husband,
    wife, and life-breath.

कृमिकीटभस्मविष्ठा दुर्गन्धिमलमूत्रकम् ।
श्लेष्मरक्तं त्वचामांसं वञ्चयेन्न वरानने ॥

kṛmikīṭabhasmaviṣṭhā durgandhimalamūtrakam /
śleṣmaraktaṃ tvacāmāṃsaṃ vañcayenna varānane //

O beautiful one, do not withhold even germs, worms, ashes, spit, stench, feces, urine, phlegm, blood, skin, flesh, and so on from the Guru; one should hold back nothing when surrendering to the Guru.

Gurugītā 30

Śaṅkara says, O Devī, some people claim, "The body is made of impurities such as germs, worms, feces, urine, phlegm, blood, flesh, skin, and so on. How can we offer such a body to the Guru?" With thoughts such as these, they don't make an offering.

This is not right. The body in which the Guru and the Self dwell can only be considered pure. There should never be any feeling of impurity about offering the body.

Seventy-two thousand channels
threading through five sheaths,
here the Self ever makes its home.
Muktananda, the wise ones see it
as the temple of the Lord.

गुरुर् ब्रह्मागुरुर् विष्णुर् गुरुर् देवो महेश्वरः ।
गुरुर् एव परब्रह्म तस्मै श्रीगुरवे नमः ॥

gurur brahmā gurur viṣṇur gurur devo maheśvaraḥ /
gurur eva parabrahma tasmai śrīgurave namaḥ //

The Guru is Brahmā. He is Viṣṇu. He is Śiva. The Guru is indeed the supreme Absolute. Salutations to the Guru.

Gurugītā 32

All the sages and seers look upon the Guru as an embodiment of the trinity of Brahmā, Viṣṇu, and Maheśvara. He is also seen as Brahman, the absolute state of transcendental bliss. There may be some people who, because of their defective understanding and ignorance of the Guru's true nature, consider this description to be untrue or an exaggeration. Just as it is said, "The mantra is real, *pūjā* is real, and God is eternal," so is this verse valid. The Guru is Maheśvara when he destroys the world of concepts stirring in his disciple's heart. The Guru is Brahmā, the creator, when he purifies the disciple's heart and sows in it the seed of the highest truth. He is Viṣṇu when he sustains and protects this newly created wisdom of yoga within the disciple.

So it is clear that the Guru is Brahmā, Viṣṇu, and Maheśvara. One could also say that the Guru is the embodiment of this trinity because, in his fullness, he pervades the entire universe. Salutations to the forms of Śrī Guru.

Of the three worlds, the three divinities,
and the three states,
the Guru is a total embodiment.
Why then roam the holy places,
O Muktananda, in search of Viṣṇu or Śiva?

हेतवे जगतामेव संसारार्णवसेतवे ।
प्रभवे सर्वविद्यानां शम्भवे गुरवे नमः ॥

hetave jagatāmeva saṃsārārṇavasetave /
prabhave sarvavidyānāṃ śambhave gurave namaḥ //

Salutations to the Guru who is Śiva, the first cause of the universe, the bridge to cross the ocean of worldliness, the source of all knowledge.

Gurugītā 33

All the great saints as well as all the different schools of spiritual philosophy have agreed that God is the root of this universe. He has created it without any motive. He is the cause; He is the effect. He is the world, and the world is His. It is He who permeates it.

This is a strange world, and the strangest thing about it is that once a person is in it, there is no escape. Its grip is like that of a python: the harder one tries to get free, the more firmly one is caught. The world is said to be an ocean, difficult to cross. But Śrī Guru serves as a bridge, enabling his disciple to go across easily. By relying on his Guru, one will face no difficulty in getting free from the world's clutches.

There are countless branches of knowledge. Among these, fourteen are considered most significant. Yet all of these branches of knowledge have value only because of the Guru; knowledge is acquired only from him.

Salutations to the Guru, who is Śiva incarnate and bestower of everything auspicious.

> Cause of the universe, bridge across the world,
> shining with the light of the Self—
> Muktananda, contemplate Nityananda,
> lord of all learning and wisdom.

अज्ञानतिमिरान्धस्य ज्ञानाञ्जनशलाकया ।
चक्षुर् उन्मीलितं येन तस्मै श्रीगुरवे नमः ॥

ajñānatimirāndhasya jñānāñjanaśalākayā /
cakṣur unmīlitaṃ yena tasmai śrīgurave namaḥ //

Salutations to the Guru, who with the collyrium of knowledge opens the eyes of one who is blinded by the darkness of ignorance.

Gurugītā 34

A person may have eyes, yet without knowledge he is considered to be spiritually blind. I bow to the Guru, who applies the lotion of awareness of the inner Self, opening the inner eye of his disciple and driving away the darkness of ignorance.

God is supreme light. He is manifest. In fact, it is very easy to see Him. Yet one can be enveloped by such thick folds of dark ignorance that for him the manifest Lord is invisible. Ignorance seems to make God unmanifest.

Applying the lotion of knowledge
to eyes blinded by ignorance,
revealing Nityananda within the heart—
Muktananda, this is the Guru, greatest of all,
showing the supreme Lord within the heart.

यत् सत्येन जागत् सत्यं यत् प्रकाशेन भाति तत् ।
यद् आनन्देन नन्दन्ति तस्मै श्रीगुरवे नमः ॥

yat satyena jagat satyaṃ yat prakāśena bhāti tat /
yad ānandena nandanti tasmai śrīgurave namaḥ //

Salutations to the Guru, whose existence causes the world to appear, whose light illumines it, whose bliss makes possible all individual experiences of joy.

Gurugītā 36

Salutations to the Guru who is saturated with bliss! He is supreme Existence and supreme Consciousness. His reality makes the world appear real. With the transcendent light of his knowledge, he illumines everything. It is he who makes us aware of what exists as well as what does not exist. He is the embodiment of total Bliss. Illumined by the effulgence of his ecstasy, all sentient and insentient beings shine with delight, and people have experiences of unconditional joy.

By his reality the world becomes real,
his love is this supreme light.
He is the inner Self, O Muktananda,
the supremely effulgent Nityananda.

यस्य स्थित्या सत्यमिदं यद् भाति भानुरूपतः ।
प्रियं पुत्रादि यत् प्रीत्या तस्मै श्रीगुरवे नमः ॥

yasya sthityā satyam idaṃ yad bhāti bhānurūpataḥ /
priyaṃ putrādi yat prītyā tasmai śrīgurave namaḥ //

Salutations to the Guru, whose state makes
this world appear real, who shines like the sun,
whose love makes relations such as sons dear.

Gurugītā 37

Salutations to Gurudev, who is the ultimate truth and the basis of all existence. In his eternal reality, this world also seems to be real. His light shines in the sun, stars, and planets. Because this blissful Guru principle is the inner Self of all, it is his love that makes our relationships with our daughter, our wife, precious to us.

The world, the sun, and the moon are real
because of your reality, O Gurudev.
Muktananda, it is the love
of the Guru Nityananda
that shines in your dear ones.

यस्य ज्ञानादिदं विश्वं न दृश्यं भिन्नभेदतः ।
सदेकरूपरूपाय तस्मै श्रीगुरवे नमः ॥

yasya jñānādidaṃ viśvaṃ na dṛśyaṃ bhinnabhedataḥ /
sadekarūparūpāya tasmai śrīgurave namaḥ //

I bow to that Lord Guru by whose knowledge
this universe ceases to appear to be filled with duality
and differences, who is of the form of truth alone.

Gurugītā 39

This universe is a wondrous mystery. It arises from a single intent of that one truth, Consciousness, yet it manifests such diversity. The universe is all just one substance, yet there is such a display of diverse forms and species, all different from one another, none resembling another.

Even though the world appears so diverse, so full of differences, once the knowledge of the Guru dawns, the supreme Absolute is all that remains. This is what is great; this is the mystery made known, that the universe is nothing but Brahman. The Guru pronounces the secret openly: right in this universe, in the form of the universe, appears the supreme Brahman. To such a Guru, who is nothing but truth incarnate, I offer my salutations.

The gift of your grace, O Guru,
bestows unity in diversity.
Muktananda, this world appearance
    is Nityananda's play,
both its reality and its unreality.

यदङ्घ्रिकमलद्वन्द्वं द्वन्द्वतापनिवारकम् ।
तारकं सर्वदाऽपद्भ्यः श्रीगुरुं प्रणमाम्यहम् ॥

yadaṅghrikamaladvandvaṃ dvandvatāpanivārakam /
tārakaṃ sarvadā'padbhyaḥ śrīguruṃ praṇamāmyaham //

Salutations to the Guru whose lotus feet eradicate the agony of dualities, who protects us from all misfortunes and calamities.

Gurugītā 43

That the supreme truth—the Guru principle—is beyond the senses is completely true. Yet when a seeker is given the gift of devotion to his Guru, all his senses are refined. And as the highest Śakti begins to flow through the senses, the extremely subtle mystery of the Guru's feet is grasped in speech and in mind and imagination. The Guru is compelled to reveal himself fully to the disciple whose tongue constantly repeats the Guru's name, the Guru-mantra, and whose mind continually meditates on the Guru's form. That disciple is able to behold the Guru's feet—the gateway to liberation. In these feet, Śiva and Śakti live as one, and through them the disciple realizes that unity. He sees Śiva and Śakti as red and white lights shining through the Guru's feet. The Guru's feet should be worshiped every day, for by this means one easily realizes the immanent and transcendent aspects of Śiva. Their luster radiates in the upper spaces of the *sahasrāra.*

Accessible and inaccessible to speech,
    mind, and imagination;
shining white and red, red and white
    are the Guru's feet.
Muktananda, worship them always.

वन्दे गुरुपदद्वन्द्वं वाङ्मनश्चित्तगोचरम् ।
श्वेतरक्तप्रभाभिन्नं शिवशक्त्यात्मकं परम् ॥

vande gurupadadvandvaṃ vāṅmanaścittagocaram /
śvetaraktaprabhābhinnaṃ śivaśaktyātmakaṃ param //

I bow to the Guru's feet, which are within the scope of speech, the *manas,* and the *citta*; which are shining with white and red effulgence; and which embody Śiva and Śakti.

Gurugītā 45

In truth, the supreme principle, the venerable Guru principle, is beyond the reach of the senses. Yet, when a seeker attains the divine blessing of devotion to the Guru, the supreme Śakti starts flowing through his senses, and his senses become subtle. Then the supreme principle can also be perceived through speech, through sense perception (*manas*), and through thought (*citta*).

The sun is the illuminator as well as the one illumined. It is the same with the Guru's feet. They appear in the higher regions of the *sahasrāra,* different even than the divine red, white, or yellow lights. They are embodiments of Śiva and Śakti and should be worshiped with great attention.

The feet of Śrī Guru,
inaccessible to speech, *manas,* or *citta,*
  are now accessible.
The feet of Śrī Guru,
beyond even the divine lights, red, white, or yellow,
  are now in these lights.
Muktananda, worship the feet of Śrī Guru.

अत्रिनेत्रः सर्वसाक्षी अचतुर्बाहुर् अच्युतः ।
अचतुर्वदनो ब्रह्मा श्रीगुरुः कथितः प्रिये ॥

atrinetraḥ sarvasākṣī acaturbāhur acyutaḥ /
acaturvadano brahmā śrīguruḥ kathitaḥ priye //

O dear one, the Lord Guru is the witness of all, though he does not have three eyes. He is Viṣṇu, the immovable one, though he does not have four arms. He is Brahmā, though he does not have four faces.

Gurugītā 47

Śrī Guru is called "the one who has the eye of knowledge"—that which is known as the third eye. He is separate from all, so he is the witness of all. Though he does not have four arms, still he is Acyuta, or Viṣṇu, the immovable one. *Cyuta* is one who falls when his time comes, one who is perishable, one who takes birth again and again. *Acyuta,* on the other hand, is one for whom there is no fall, no shift of any kind; one who remains perfect and steady. The Guru creates a new knowledge of the Self in the heart of the disciple; this is why he is called Brahmā.

श्रीगुरोः परमं रूपं विवेकचक्षुषोऽमृतम् ।
मन्दभाग्या न पश्यन्ति अन्धाः सूर्योदयं यथा ॥

śrīguroḥ paramaṃ rūpaṃ vivekacakṣuṣo'mṛtam /
mandabhāgyā na paśyanti andhāḥ sūryodayaṃ yathā //

For one who has acquired the eye of discrimination, the supreme form of the Guru is like pure nectar. But just as the blind cannot see the sunrise, an unfortunate person cannot perceive the Guru's glory.

Gurugītā 49

The Guru's form is supremely enchanting. It is the endless treasure of Citi's loveliness. It is the form of the formless. The world is beautiful because it is pervaded by the Guru's inner beauty. Only a seeker whose inner eye has been opened through meditation is able to perceive the Guru's form and drink the nectar of its beauty.

One who lacks devotion to the Guru is utterly unfortunate. Just as a blind man cannot see the sunrise, so such a one cannot behold the Guru's form.

He is liberated while still living
who sees the inner radiance of Śrī Guru,
shimmering with the conscious lights
of red, white, blue, and yellow.

श्रीनाथचरणद्वन्द्वं यस्यां दिशि विराजते ।
तस्यै दिशे नमस्कुर्याद् भक्त्या प्रतिदिनं प्रिये ।।

śrīnāthacaraṇadvandvaṃ yasyāṃ diśi virājate /
tasyai diśe namaskuryād bhaktyā pratidinaṃ priye //

O beloved, bow with devotion every day
in the direction of the Guru's feet.

Gurugītā 50

The Guru is Existence, Consciousness, and Bliss. In his purest essence, he is without form and quality. Yet the disciple has a form and also qualities. He has a body. How can the formless one communicate knowledge of the Self to one who has a form? It is to impart knowledge of the Self to the disciple that the formless takes a form. The Guru does this to awaken his disciples, to bestow yogic knowledge, and uplift the world.

Thus a disciple should remember his Guru's feet and bow humbly in their direction. He could also kneel at his Guru's feet in his inner mind.

Supreme Śiva, the Guru, dwells in the center of the *sahasrāra.* To focus one's attention there and to bow is the highest salutation. However, one who is ardently devoted to the Guru will receive the blessed touch of his feet wherever the devotee's folded hands touch the earth.

In all directions,
in the whole universe,
over the surface of the earth
dwell the holy feet of Nityananda.
O Muktananda, bow to them.

तस्यै दिशे सततम् अञ्जलिरेष आर्ये
प्रक्षिप्यते मुखरितो मधुपैर् बुद्धैश्च ।
जागर्ति यत्र भगवान् गुरुचक्रवर्ती
विश्वोदयप्रलयनाटकनित्यसाक्षी ॥

tasyai diśe satatam añjalireṣa ārye
prakṣipyate mukharito madhupair budhaiśca /
jāgarti yatra bhagavān gurucakravartī
viśvodayapralayanāṭakanityasākṣī //

O noble one, like humming bees attracted by lotuses, the wise always offer their obeisance with folded hands at the lotus feet of the Guru. They bow in the direction of the sovereign cause of the world cycle, Bhagawan Śrī Guru, who is always awake, witnessing the creation and dissolution of the universe.

Gurugītā 51

O those who thirst after the nectar of devotion to the Guru! O devotees who want to drink the nectar from the Guru's lotus feet, which are in full bloom with the rich fragrance of the knowledge of yoga!

Know that the Guru lives in the blue radiance that is blazing in the center of the upper regions of the *sahasrāra*. He is the transcendental one who never sleeps, who ever keeps awake, witnessing all in supreme bliss. To offer him the flowers of meditation is true meditation and the highest worship. One who practices the yoga of meditation makes his offering of flowers there.

At the center of the *sahasrāra*,
at the seat of Consciousness
where Nityananda dwells,
O Muktananda, offer your flowers
of meditation there,
with love, with hands folded.

यत्पादरेणुकणिका कापि संसारवरिधेः ।
सेतुबन्धायते नाथं देशिकं तमुपास्महे ।।

yatpādareṇukaṇikā kāpi saṃsāravaridheḥ /
setubandhāyate nāthaṃ deśikaṃ tam upāsmahe //

Even a single particle of the dust of the Guru's feet
forms a bridge strong enough to cross the ocean of change.
One should seek to attain Lord Guru.

Gurugītā 55

The vast ocean of *saṃsāra* is very hard to cross. But with the support of even a single particle of the dust of the Guru's lotus feet, it can be crossed with ease. The remembrance of the Guru's feet is an absolutely dependable bridge. After a seeker has taken refuge at the Guru's sacred feet, those things that bound him before to birth and death, to pleasure and pain, now bring liberation. The world begins to appear as it really is—a visible image of the inner spirit. Worship the Guru as the inner Self.

Do not let the ocean of the world
of change frighten you; be calm.
O Muktananda, ascend the great bridge
of Nityananda
and happily proceed on your journey.

यस्माद् अनुग्रहं लब्ध्वा महदज्ञानमुत्सृजेत् ।
तस्मै श्रीदेशिकेन्द्राय नमश्चाभीष्टसिद्धये ॥

yasmād anugrahaṃ labdhvā mahadajñānam utsṛjet /
tasmai śrīdeśikendrāya namaścābhīṣṭasiddhaye //

By receiving his grace, great ignorance is destroyed.
Salutations to Śrī Gurudeva for the attainment
of the desired object.

Gurugītā 56

Bestowing grace is the great mission of the Guru.

यस्य स्मरणमात्रेण ज्ञानम् उत्पद्यते स्वयम् ।
य एव सर्वसम्प्राप्तिस् तस्मै श्रीगुरवे नमः ॥

yasya smaraṇamātreṇa jñānam utpadyate svayam /
ya eva sarvasamprāptis tasmai śrīgurave namaḥ //

By whose mere remembrance knowledge dawns by itself,
who himself is the whole attainment, to that Śrī Gurudeva I bow.

Gurugītā 69

In truth, a human being has no name or designation. He is neither man nor woman nor an individual soul, neither high nor low. Each person stands within the scope of his or her own understanding.

Consider a woman: she is daughter to one, mother to another, wife to someone else, and a grandmother to a fourth. What role she plays in any moment is determined by the particular thoughts or feelings she holds.

Whatever awareness a person holds, whatever arises from inside, that constitutes his or her understanding.

If a disciple is true, it is easy for that disciple to make the knowledge of the Guru dawn spontaneously within, simply by the inner remembrance of Śrī Guru. Everything is attained by contemplating a Guru who is himself perfect. To that auspicious Guru I bow.

By meditation on a bee,
a larva easily becomes a bee.
Muktananda, meditate on Śrī Guru
and receive the knowledge of Nityananda with ease.

अनेकजन्मसम्प्राप्तसर्वकर्मविदाहिने ।
स्वात्मज्ञानप्रभावेण तस्मै श्रीगुरवे नमः ॥

anekajanmasamprāptasarvakarmavidāhine /
svātmajñānaprabhāveṇa tasmai śrīgurave namaḥ //

Salutations to the Guru, who by the power of Self-knowledge burns up all the karma accumulated through countless lives.

Gurugītā 73

Because the embodied soul has existed from time without beginning, the accumulated store of its past karma is inconceivably vast. It is past karma that causes happiness and sorrow, pleasure and pain, in different ways. Enchained in the shackles of karma, the individual soul is born, dies, is reborn and dies again and again; transmigrating through different life-forms, high and low; exhausting his past karma and creating new karma for the future. He remains bound to the wheel of karma, sorely afflicted.

When the Guru's grace is received and the fire of knowledge is kindled within, a person's karmas are burned. Awareness of the Self has the power to annihilate all karma. I bow again and again to the Guru who bestows Self-knowledge.

O Muktananda, the stored karmas
of innumerable lifetimes will be easily consumed
when the fire of Self-knowledge
is kindled through Nityananda's grace.

ज्ञानं विज्ञानसहितं लभ्यते गुरुभक्तितः ।
गुरोः परतरं नास्ति ध्येयोऽसौ गुरुमार्गिभिः ॥

jñānaṃ vijñānasahitaṃ labhyate gurubhaktitaḥ /
guroḥ parataraṃ nāsti dhyeyo'sau gurumārgibhiḥ //

By devotion to the Guru, one obtains knowledge as well as realization. There is nothing higher than the Guru. Therefore, the devotees of the Guru should meditate on him.

Gurugītā 81

Devotion to the Guru is the wish-fulfilling cow, the wish-fulfilling tree, and the wish-fulfilling jewel. *Jñāna* is intellectual knowledge of truth, while *vijñāna* is direct experiential awareness of truth. Knowledge, experience, and the highest wisdom are gained with ease and without strain by devotion to the Guru. The devotees of the Guru should meditate on him alone. For them there is no other deity.

A larva becomes a bee
by meditation on the bee.
O Muktananda, become fulfilled
by worshiping Nityananda,
the embodiment of *jñāna* and *vijñāna*.

गुरोः कृपाप्रसादेन ब्रह्मविष्णुसदाशिवः ।
समर्थाः प्रभवादौ च केवलं गुरुसेवया ॥

guroḥ kṛpāprasādena brahmaviṣṇusadāśivāḥ /
samarthāḥ prabhavādau ca kevalaṃ gurusevayā //

Brahmā, Viṣṇu, and Sadāśivā become capable of creation, sustenance, and dissolution only through the grace of the Guru; the state of final Oneness is attained only through service to the Guru.

Gurugītā 83

What is greater than the Self? There is no deity greater than the Self, no miracle greater than the Self, no friend dearer than the Self, no mantra greater than the Self, no place of pilgrimage greater than the Self; nor is there a Guru greater than the Self. The inner Self dwelling in all is the chief, supreme Guru. Without the grace of the inner Self, there is no outer Guru. The various gods and goddesses derive their powers to create the universe only by the grace of the Self.

Root of all powers,
key to all sadhanas,
seed of the creation,
O Muktananda, is Nityananda.

यस्मिन् सृष्टिस्थितिध्वंसनिग्रहानुग्रहात्मकम् ।
कृत्यं पञ्चविधं शश्वद् भासते तं नमाम्यहम् ॥

yasmin sṛṣṭisthitidhvaṃsanigrahānugrahātmakam /
kṛtyaṃ pañcavidhaṃ śaśvad bhāsate taṃ namāmyaham //

I bow to the Guru, the author of the five eternal cosmic processes—creation, sustenance, dissolution, control, and award of grace.

Gurugītā 94

Like supreme Śiva, the Guru constantly performs the five cosmic functions. First, creation. He creates the awareness of the Self of all in the inner spaces of his disciple's heart.

Second, sustenance. Out of compassion, he transmits his spiritual energy into the disciple. He inspires the disciple to constantly contemplate this new, all-embracing Consciousness, finally establishing him permanently in it.

Third, destruction. He destroys the world of ignorance that his disciple had inhabited before their meeting.

Fourth, control. He rescues his disciple's mind from uncontrolled dualistic and negative thinking.

Fifth, grace. He showers his grace upon his disciple abundantly, transmitting his Śakti into him. By this supreme initiation, the disciple experiences an inner awakening and becomes aware of his own divinity.

I bow again and again to the auspicious Guru, who continually manifests his divine play, performing his fivefold function.

Muktananda, turn away from false gurus.
Clasp the feet of your Master, Nityananda—
the creator, sustainer, destroyer,
controller, and bestower of grace.

एवम् विधं गुरुं ध्यात्वा ज्ञानम् उत्पद्यते स्वयम् ।
तत्सद्गुरुप्रसादेन मुक्तोऽहमिति भावयेत् ॥

evam vidhaṃ guruṃ dhyātvā jñānam utpadyate svayam /
tatsadguruprasādena mukto'hamiti bhāvayet //

By meditating on the Guru, one gains knowledge spontaneously.
By the grace of the *sadguru,* become aware: "I am liberated."

Gurugītā 98

Know Gurudev to be Mahādev and Viṣṇudev. He is Nārāyaṇa, Śakti, Sarasvatī, the perfect deity, and Lord of all *yajñas.* He is also the primordial supreme power behind the universe, that pure Consciousness that is the Self of all. When one meditates on the Guru with this awareness, perfect knowledge arises from within. This is the same knowledge that came to great sages like Vyāsa and Vasiṣṭha, and great saints like Jñāneśvar and Tukārām.

One who meditates on the Guru does not have to depend on external sources for knowledge. The self-existent inner treasure of wisdom becomes available to him of its own accord. He achieves the awareness: "I am liberated, I am perfect, I have attained everything."

Muktananda, when your Master, Nityananda,
is the God of all gods,
the inner essence of all *yajñas,*
why should you adore other deities?

गुरुदर्शितमार्गेण मनःशुद्धिं तु कारयेत् ।
अनित्यं खण्डयेत् सर्वं यत् किञ्चिदात्मगोचरम् ॥

gurudarśitamārgeṇa manaḥśuddhiṃ tu kārayet /
anityaṃ khaṇḍayet sarvaṃ yat kiñcidātmagocaram //

Purify your mind by following the Guru's path. Detach yourself from all transient things perceived by the mind and senses.

Gurugītā 99

There is only one way shown by the Guru—the way of shaktipat, the way of grace, of benediction, of compassion. When a seeker is blessed by the Guru, his entire body is transformed anew, and he begins to move through worlds previously unknown to him. The Guru's guidance, which is charged with his Śakti, works within the disciple, and his mind is totally cleansed. As devotion to the Guru blazes in his heart, all his impurities are consumed. An aspirant should renounce the paths of affectation and hypocrisy and cling to the path of grace.

Since inner awakening is the same for all,
why should Muktananda turn away
from Nityananda's grace?
He would become trapped in show and pretense.

ज्ञेयं सर्वस्वरूपं च ज्ञानं च मन उच्यते ।
ज्ञानं ज्ञेयसमं कुर्यान् नान्यः पन्था द्वितीयकः ॥

jñeyaṃ sarvasvarūpaṃ ca jñānaṃ ca mana ucyate /
jñānaṃ jñeyasamaṃ kuryān nānyaḥ panthā dvitīyakaḥ //

The Self, which is the essential nature of all things, is called the object of knowledge, and the mind is called knowledge itself. Realize the identity of knowledge with the object of knowledge. There is no other way to liberation.

Gurugītā 100

The universe is full of Citi. Citi has become everything. Nothing that is not Citi can exist. Whatever is, whatever has been or will be—all is Citi. Rāma is Citi, the world is Citi. Day is Citi and night is Citi.

The knower and the known and also knowledge are all Citi. So, too, are the mind, intellect, and ego. With this understanding, it is true wisdom to realize that the mind is not only knowledge, but also the thing known. There is no path other than this to equal vision.

> Actor, action, and the instrument of action;
> perceiver, perception, and the perceived;
> everything animate and inanimate—
> Muktananda, these are your beloved Nityananda.

यावत् कल्पान्तको देहस् तावदेव गुरुं स्मरेत् ।
गुरुलोपो न कर्तव्यः स्वच्छन्दो यदि वा भवेत् ॥

yāvat kalpāntako dehas tāvadeva guruṃ smaret /
gurulopo na kartavyaḥ svacchando yadi vā bhavet //

Continue to remember the Guru until the end of time, as long as the body lasts. Never forget the Guru, even on attaining the state of boundless freedom.

Gurugītā 102

The Guru is the wish-fulfilling cow, the wish-fulfilling tree, the wish-fulfilling jewel—what need is there to worship another? Be absorbed in remembrance of the Guru as long as breath remains in your body.

A yogi in the highest state has attained complete independence and total freedom. In that state a yogi is no longer subject to outer constraint, rules, convention, tradition, or norm. He lives and moves freely without compulsion. But even when he has reached this state of boundless freedom, he should not cease being faithful and devoted to his Guru.

Continue to worship the Guru
as long as the body has life.
Muktananda, failure in *gurubhakti*
is the same as descent into hell.

श्रुतिस्मृती अविज्ञाय केवलं गुरुसेवकाः ।
ते वै संन्यासिनः प्रोक्ता इतरे वेषधारिणः ॥

śrutismṛtī avijñāya kevalaṃ gurusevakāḥ /
te vai sannyāsinaḥ proktā itare veṣadhāriṇaḥ //

Those who are dedicated to *gurusevā* alone, even without having knowledge of the Vedas and the Upaniṣads, are true renunciants. The rest are merely wearing the robes of a *sannyāsī.*

Gurugītā 108

The Vedas and the Upaniṣads, which are called *śrutis,* along with all the other scriptures, are the utterances of Śrī Guru. Without the Guru, there is no knowledge, no light of knowledge, no possibility of mastering yoga. All knowledge arises from the Guru and from the Guru alone.

Service to the Guru is the root of all knowledge. With the understanding that the Guru is the source of all, the true aspirant renounces other duties and adopts *gurusevā* as his supreme dharma.

Such renunciants, having surrendered completely to the Guru, truly deserve the title "the supreme one among renunciants."

No one can become a renunciant merely by adopting the robes of a *sannyāsī.* A person who indulges in such appearances is just wearing costumes. He leads an utterly bound existence.

The Vedas and Purāṇas,
aphorisms and commentaries,
are contained in the words of the Guru.
O Muktananda, renounce scriptural pursuits.
Remember Śrī Guru's name
and become a perfect renunciant.

गुरुध्यानं तथा कृत्वा स्वयं ब्रह्ममयो भवेत् ।
पिण्डे पदे तथा रूपे मुक्तोऽसौ नात्र संशयः ॥

gurudhyānaṃ tathā kṛtvā svayaṃ brahmamayo bhavet /
piṇḍe pade tathā rūpe mukto'sau nātra saṃśayaḥ //

A disciple himself becomes divine by meditating on the Guru. There is no doubt that one whose Kuṇḍalinī is awake, *prāṇa* steady, and who sees the Blue Pearl is liberated.

Gurugītā 119

One comes to be like that on which one meditates. If you think continually of sin you will become a sinner; if you think of ghosts you will become one. If you worship God you become God. It follows that you can become the Guru by constant remembrance of him. By means of unceasing meditation on the Guru, a seeker can easily attain oneness with the Absolute.

Piṇḍa is Kuṇḍalinī Śakti. The sleeping Kuṇḍalinī is awakened by meditation on the Guru, and the seeker is liberated from the bondage of Her coils. *Pada* is *Haṃsa,* or swan, the state of supreme discrimination. In the course of meditation on the Guru, the seeker becomes aware of his identity with the Guru: *So'ham,* "I am That." *Rūpa* is the supreme Blue Pearl. In time the seeker has a vision of the Blue Pearl in meditation, and later he passes beyond that into the pure and unstained supra-transcendental state. He becomes fully liberated. These are real experiences and are not to be doubted. You can have them yourself through meditation.

You are surrendering all sadhanas
when you meditate on Nityananda.
Kuṇḍalinī will awaken, O Muktananda,
bringing the dawn of the blue
and the sound of *So'ham.*

NOTES

1. The Indian tradition identifies the four goals of life as dharma (righteousness); *artha* (abundance); *kāma* (pleasure); and *mokṣa* (liberation).

2. Baba Muktananda also uses the term *Blue Person* when referring to this form of the supreme reality that grants a yogi the final vision. In *Play of Consciousness* he writes of "the Blue Lord, whose nature is *sat chit ānanda* — Being, Consiousness, and Bliss. Seeing Him, the *sādhaka* enjoys happiness free from duality. He acquires supreme knowledge, free from doubts, and knowledge of the identity of all things."

3. Here Baba Muktananda makes reference to nineteen of the principles (*tattvas*) that Indian philosophers identify as comprising the universe. A full description of the *tattvas* is given by J. C. Chatterji in *Kashmir Shaivism* (Albany: State University of New York Press, 1986). For a discussion of these "categories of existence," see Mark S. G. Dyczkowski, *The Doctrine of Vibration: An Analysis of the Doctrines and Practices of Kashmir Shaivism* (Albany: State University of New York Press, 1987).

4. In describing the creation of the universe, *sāṃkhya,* the philosophical foundation for Patañjali's *Yoga Sūtra,* identifies twenty-five distinct principles of existence (*tattvas*) that compose all aspects of manifestation. Other philosophies incorporate this construct, adding further *tattvas* to describe subtle components of creation.

5. In the Hindu tradition, the three *guṇas,* the three qualities of nature, are thought to form the universe in the way that three strands of hemp might be interwoven to form a rope. All of creation is said to be composed of varying combinations of the *guṇas*—*sattva* (purity), *rajas* (passion), and *tamas* (inertia). One who rises above these transcends the boundaries of the world. For a description of the *guṇas* in relation to sadhana, see Swami Chidvilasananda's *The Yoga of Discipline* (South Fallsburg, New York: SYDA Foundation, 1996).

6. The sages of Vedānta say that the *ātman,* here called the "conscious spirit," is encased in five concentric coverings (*kośas*) of increasing subtlety: physical matter, vital energy, mind, intelligence, and bliss.

7. In the Indian scriptures, the world is said to be comprised of five elemental realities: earth, water, fire, air, and ether (or space). For further discussion, see Gerald J. Larson, *Classical Sāṃkhya: An Interpretation of Its History and Meaning* (Delhi, India: Motilal Banarsidass, 1972).

8. In the Āyurvedic system of medicine, the seven bodily constituents are blood, bone, fat, flesh, lymphatic fluid, marrow, and semen.

9. According to the Kashmir Śaivite view of creation, which posits thirty-six categories of existence, Sadāśiva is the *tattva* in which the universe first appears as an idea in the mind of God, and earth is the final *tattva*, the level of manifestation most deeply imbedded in form. What is being said here is that with the grace of the spiritual Master, one experiences union with all the levels of creation. For a discussion of the relationship of Śiva to Sadāśiva, see Paul Muller-Ortega's *The Triadic Heart of Śiva: Kaula Tantricism of Abhinavagupta in the Non-Dual Shaivism of Kashmir* (Albany: State University of New York Press, 1989).

10. Here the *Vijñānabhairava* is describing the path of Kuṇḍalinī as She makes Her way through successively higher centers of energy. She begins with the root center, the *mūlādhāra*, and, moving past certain physical points of reference, She travels up to the topmost center in the crown of the head, the *brahmarandhra*. For a discussion of Swami Muktananda's description of the inner journey of *śakti*, see the chapter on Kuṇḍalinī in Douglas Renfrew Brooks, Swami Durgananda, et al., *Meditation Revolution: A History and Theology of the Siddha Yoga Lineage* (South Fallsburg, New York: Agama Press, 1997).

11. While at the highest levels of sound, the *praṇava*, the primordial vibration, is one, at the *vaikharī* or spoken level, each of the various traditions has its own way of expressing it. For further discussion of the understanding of mantra, see Andre Padoux, *Vāc: The Concept of the Word in Selected Hindu Tantras* (Albany: State University of New York Press, 1990). For an elaboration of *praṇava* and other mantras, see Douglas Renfrew Brooks, *The Secret of Three Cities: An Introduction to Hindu Śākta Tantrism* (Chicago: University of Chicago Press, 1990).

NOTE ON THE SANSKRIT

For the reader's convenience, the Sanskrit and Hindi terms most frequently used in Siddha Yoga literature and courses appear throughout the text in roman type with simple transliteration: *śaktipāta,* for instance, is shaktipat; *sādhana* is sadhana, and so on. Otherwise the standard international transliteration scheme for South Asian languages has been used.

For the readers not familiar with Sanskrit, the following is a guide for pronunciation:

Vowels

Sanskrit vowels are categorized as either long or short. In English transliteration, long vowels are indicated with a macron, a horizontal line over the vowel, with the exception of the *e* and the *ai,* and the *o* and the *au,* which are always long.

Short:
a as in *cup*
i as in *give*
u as in *full*
ṛ as in *written*

Long:
ā as in *calm*
ī as in *seen*
ū as in *school*
e as in *era*
o as in *know*
ai as in *aisle*
au as in *cow*

Consonants

The main differences between Sanskrit and English pronunciation of consonants are in the aspirated and retroflexive letters.

The aspirated letters have a definite *h* sound. The Sanskrit letter *kh* is pronounced as in *inkhorn;* the *th* as in *boathouse;* the *ph* as in *loophole.*

The retroflexes are pronounced with the tip of the tongue touching the hard palate; *ṭ,* for instance, is pronounced as in *ant; ḍ* as in *end.*

The sibilants, which are often confused, are *ś, ṣ,* and *s.* The *ś* is pronounced as *sh* but with the tongue touching the soft palate; the *ṣ* as *sh* with the tongue touching the hard palate; the *s* as in *history.*

Other distinctive consonants are these:

c as in *church*
ch as in *pitch-hook*
ñ as in *canyon*

ṃ is a strong nasal
ḥ is a strong aspiration

GLOSSARY

of words not defined in the text

ājñā cakra: the spiritual center between the eyebrows; the seat of the Guru

anāhata cakra: the spiritual center located in the region of the heart

ātman: the soul, the inner Self

bhairavī mudrā: also known as *khecarī mudrā*; a stance in which the attention is directed inward even though the eyes are open

bhakta: devotee

Brahman: the Absolute; the all-pervasive supreme reality

brahmarandhra: the topmost spiritual center

gurubhakti: devotion for the spiritual Master

Gurudev: a term of address signifying the spiritual Master who has attained oneness with the Lord

gurusevā: service to the spiritual Master

japa: mantra repetition

jīva: the individual bound soul

kriyā: a gross or subtle purificatory movement initiated by the awakened Kuṇḍalinī

madhyadaśa: the still space between the inbreath and the outbreath

mahāyogī: a great practitioner of yoga

manipūra cakra: the spiritual center located in the navel region

mudrā: an advanced hatha yoga technique, practiced to keep the *prāṇa* in the body

mūlādhāra cakra: the spiritual center at the base of the spine

prāṇaśakti: the life force

praṇava: the primal mantra; *Oṃ*

prāṇāyāma: yogic breathing exercises to stabilize the vital force

pūjā: a ritual worship

rajas: the quality of activity and passion

sādhaka: a spiritual seeker

sadhana: a spiritual discipline or path; spiritual practices

sahasrāra: the spiritual center at the crown of the head

śāktopāya: the path to Śiva-consciousness through the use of the mind

samādhi: the state of final absorption in God

śāmbhavopāya, the *śāmbhava* way: the sudden emergence of Śiva-consciousness by a mere hint from the Guru

saṃsāra: the world of birth, mutability, and death

sannyāsī: a monk

sattva: the quality of purity and light

siddhis: supernatural powers

sūtra: aphorism

tamas: the quality of darkness and inertia

Tantra *śāstra*: a body of Śaivite scripture

tattva: a principle of creation

Temple, the: The Bhagawan Nityananda Temple at Gurudev Siddha Peeth, the Siddha Yoga ashram in Ganeshpuri, India

Vedas, the: ancient scriptures of India

yajña: fire ritual; sacrifice

by
SWAMI MUKTANANDA

Play of Consciousness

In this intimate and powerful portrait, Swami Muktananda describes his own journey to Self-realization, revealing the process of transformation he experienced under the guidance of his Guru, Bhagawan Nityananda.

Secret of the Siddhas

For thousands of years, the teachings of the Siddha Masters have been handed down from Guru to disciple. Here Swami Muktananda introduces us to the extraordinary lineage of Siddhas and interprets some basic tenets of Vedānta and Kashmir Śaivism, two philosophical schools at the heart of Siddha Yoga.

I Am That: The Science of Hamsa from the Vijnana-Bhairava

The secret of *Hamsa,* the awareness of the natural mantra of the breath, is revealed most clearly in verse 24 of the the great Śaivite text, *Vijñānabhairava.* In his commentary, Baba Muktananda leads us step by step into the mysteries of this potent form of mantra repetition.

Bhagawan Nityananda of Ganeshpuri

He rarely spoke, but a brief sentence from him spoke volumes, guiding the fortunate listener across the sea of illusion. This volume on the life of Bhagawan Nityananda is filled with the observations, thoughts, and offerings of praise—compiled from many sources, over many years—of his successor, the Siddha Master Swami Muktananda.

Mukteshwari

Baba Muktananda guides us through the stages of the spiritual path, inviting us to throw off our limitations and join him in the state of total freedom. These autobiographical verses, among Baba's earliest writings, are now offered in this new, single-volume edition, featuring nine photos of Baba.

by Swami Chidvilasananda

Enthusiasm

"Be filled with enthusiasm and sing God's glory" is the theme of this collection of talks given by Gurumayi Chidvilasananda. In these pages, she inspires us to let the radiance of enthusiasm shine through every action, every thought, every minute of our lives. This, Gurumayi says, is singing God's glory.

The Yoga of Discipline

"From the standpoint of the spiritual path," Swami Chidvilasananda says, "the term *discipline* is alive with the joyful expectancy of divine fulfillment." In this series of talks on practicing and cultivating discipline of the senses, Gurumayi shows us how this practice brings great joy.

My Lord Loves a Pure Heart: The Yoga of Divine Virtues

Fearlessness, reverence, compassion, freedom from anger—Gurumayi describes how these magnificent virtues are an integral part of our true nature. The list of virtues introduced in this volume is based on chapter 16 of the *Bhagavadgītā*.

Inner Treasures

"Every heart blazes with divine light," Gurumayi says. "Every heart trembles with divine love." In these inspiring talks, she offers us practical ways to cultivate the inner treasures: peace, joy, and love.

The Magic of the Heart: Reflections on Divine Love

In these profound and tender reflections on divine love, Gurumayi Chidvilasananda makes it clear that the supreme Heart is a place we must get to know. It is here, she tells us, in the interior of the soul, that "the Lord reveals Himself every second of the day."

You may learn more about the teachings
and practices of Siddha Yoga meditation by contacting:

SYDA Foundation
P.O. Box 600, 371 Brickman Rd.
South Fallsburg, NY 12779-0600, USA

Tel: (914) 434-2000

or

Gurudev Siddha Peeth
P.O. Ganeshpuri
PIN 401 206
District Thana
Maharashtra, India

For further information on books in print by Swami Muktananda and Swami Chidvilasananda, and editions in translation, please contact:

Siddha Yoga Meditation Bookstore
P.O. Box 600, 371 Brickman Rd.
South Fallsburg, NY 12779-0600, USA

Tel: (914) 434-2000 ext. 1700
Call toll-free from the United States and Canada: 888-422-3334
FAX toll-free from the United States and Canada: 888-422-3339